Queering Iberia

Iberian Masculinities at the Margins

EDITED BY

Josep M. Armengol-Carrera

PETER LANG
New York • Washington, D.C./Baltimore • Bern
Frankfurt • Berlin • Brussels • Vienna • Oxford

Library of Congress Cataloging-in-Publication Data

Queering Iberia: Iberian masculinities at the margins /
edited by Josep M. Armengol-Carrera.
p. cm. — (Masculinity studies: literary and cultural representations; v. 2)
Includes bibliographical references.
1. Queer theory—Iberian Peninsula. 2. Masculinity—Iberian Peninsula.
3. Machismo—Iberian Peninsula. 4. Iberian Peninsula—
Civilization. I. Armengol, Josep M.
HQ76.3.I155Q44   306.76010946—dc23   2011046964
ISBN 978-1-4331-1851-7 (hardcover)
ISBN 978-1-4539-0550-0 (e-book)
ISSN 2161-2692

Bibliographic information published by **Die Deutsche Nationalbibliothek**.
Die Deutsche Nationalbibliothek lists this publication in the "Deutsche
Nationalbibliografie"; detailed bibliographic data is available
on the Internet at http://dnb.d-nb.de/.

Grateful acknowledgment is made to the
University of Castilla-La Mancha for its financial support.

The paper in this book meets the guidelines for permanence and durability
of the Committee on Production Guidelines for Book Longevity
of the Council of Library Resources.

© 2012 Peter Lang Publishing, Inc., New York
29 Broadway, 18th floor, New York, NY 10006
www.peterlang.com

Printed in Germany

Contents

Introduction

Josep M. Armengol-Carrera
University of Castilla-La Mancha

As its title indicates, the present volume aims to "queer" Iberian masculinities at the "margins." Because of its focus, the collection is bound to question a number of widespread assumptions and long-held beliefs. First of all, it challenges the recurrent association of Hispanic cultures with the *macho* archetype, in general, and with the heterosexist foundations of such archetype, in particular. Admittedly, the Iberian Peninsula has produced some of the most compelling and enduring male stereotypes in Western literature and culture, including eponymous characters such as El Cid and Don Juan and iconic personages such as the bullfighter or the hidalgo, among others. Thus, both Spain and Hispanic cultures have long been associated with the conventional notions of *machismo* and the *macho* that originated in medieval Iberia.

Nevertheless, constructions of masculinity in the Iberian Peninsula and in Iberian cultures as they developed beyond the Peninsula go far beyond these figures. In the Catalan-speaking territories, in Galicia, in the Basque Country, as well as in the Americas, other styles and figurations of masculinity exist below the radar of the medieval, Renaissance, and Baroque texts that gave rise to this gallery of characters. And perhaps in Spanish language literature, Don Quixote can already be said to "queer" traditional images of *macho bravado*, following on the heels of his Catalan counterpart, Tirant lo Blanc.

This book will thus focus on both tracing and revisiting these archetypes of masculinity from ancient Iberia to the present, by placing them in the context of the divergent counter-images that exist, and have always existed, below the radar. The volume will be especially concerned with the exploration of alternative models for being a man which examine or challenge the traditional links between machismo and Hispanic culture, and/or "deviate" from the canonical models of manhood. Therefore, the essays in this collection investigate both the construction and de-construction of masculinity in Iberian cultures and literatures, from different genres and historical periods, from different disciplines (literary studies, film studies, art, religion, visual culture, etc.) and methodological perspectives (masculinity studies, feminist theory, queer studies, cultural studies, etc.). We are particularly interested in re-visions of Iberian masculinities, especially as they are manifested in Catalonia, the Basque country, and Galicia, as well as in the Americas.[1] We hope that rethinking masculinities from these counterpoints will contribute different perspectives on the topic, and that by exploring Iberian cultures through masculinities we will understand new aspects of the relationships among these cultures. While there exists a large number of texts on *machismo* in different Hispanic cultures,[2] and while several studies have set out to study non-normative gender and sexual patterns in Iberian literature and cultures,[3] fewer scholars seem to have explored the possibility of "queering" Iberia from both the sexual *and* cultural (i.e., national) margins. In so doing, *Queering Iberia* attempts not only to underline the intrinsically "margin-al" elements of Iberian literature and culture, both in sexual and national(ist) terms, but also to explore the (conflicting) relationship between sexual and cultural "deviance." Ultimately, then, the book problematizes any clear-cut distinctions between the "norm-al" and the "margin-al," questioning the classic divisions between normative and non-normative sexualities, as well as between the cultural "center" and "the peripheries," the "metropolis" and "the borderlands."

The first chapter, by José Cartagena-Calderón, sets out to "queer" Iberia by exploring the homoerotic elements of most visual representations of Saint Sebastian during (and since) the early modern period in Spain. While the widespread popularity of the cult devoted to Saint Sebastian in the Hispanic world has, through the centuries, ensured a constant production of textual and visual images, literary critics and art historians have hardly granted a deserving scholarly interest to the social and cultural dimensions of his treatment in early modern Hispanic letters and the visual arts. In fact, unlike other popular saints like Saint Joseph, whose cult and imagery played a complex role in the construction of norms of masculinity in Imperial Spain, no comprehensive study has ever been carried out from any perspective on the imaginative representation of Saint Sebastian during any period of Spanish history and its vast Empire. Although Saint Sebastian has had various religious and gendered incarnations throughout history from plague saint in the Middle Ages to decadent and androgynous icon in the late nineteenth century, in contemporary popular culture he is regarded as the unofficial patron saint of homosexual men, much to the discomfort of modern church authorities. Drawing on a rich array of sixteenth- and seventeenth-century sources from the Iberian Peninsula and colonial Latin America, Cartagena provides textual and pictorial support that suggests that Saint Sebastian's representation in literature and visual culture fostered homoerotic implications in the early modern period and beyond. Cartagena also reflects on the broader implications of these findings for the history of sexuality, masculinity, and non-normative forms of desire in its Spanish context. In particular, Cartagena traces the (homoerotic) influence of Saint Sebastian on early modern Spanish and Catalan literature, focusing on Joanot Martorell's association of the masculine hero of his late fifteenth-century chivalry novel *Tirant lo Blanc* with the figure of Saint Sebastian in a homoerotic context.

If Cartagena "queers" Catalan literature by associating its best-known knight with homoeroticism, in the next chapter Begoña Regueiro-Salgado sets out to challenge the Don Juan myth of masculinity by focusing on the literature of two other national and cultural "peripheries" —namely, Galicia and the Basque country. More specifically, she concentrates on re-visions of masculinity in Spain during the second half of the nineteenth century, as presented in a (selected) number of literary works by peripheral Spanish Second Romantics. The chapter pays special attention to the work of two Spanish Romantic writers, Antonio Trueba and Rosalía de Castro, who came from the Basque Country and Galicia, respectively. Linking their literary production to the rise in nationalism in their communities at the time, Regueiro demonstrates how both authors were centrally concerned with showing the rest of Spain the particular characteristics of their regions, including, as we shall see, their specific gendered behaviors, which differed from the then dominant models in Spain for a number of social, cultural, historical, and political reasons.

Focusing as well on the Galician context, the next chapter, by Danny M. Barreto, explores the sexual and national implications behind the case of Manuel Blanco Romasanta, the Galician lycanthrope who claimed the lives of at least thirteen victims in the first half of the nineteenth century and whose story passed instantly from history to myth. Interpreting the tale in a historical and regionalist context, Barreto discusses how the tale of the "Hombre lobo de Allariz" has allowed writers and film directors to queer conceptions of masculinity and Spanish identity. Building on Judith Halberstam's work on Gothic monsters, he shows how this nineteenth-century werewolf blurs the boundaries between history and fiction, male and female, heterosexuality and homosexuality, as well as Galicia and Spain. In so doing, Barreto concludes that, for more than a century, the werewolf's excesses and transgressive ambiguities have helped articulate a Galician identity.

Moving from Galicia to the Basque country, the next chapter, by Jaume Martí-Olivella, will focus on the politics of masculine narrative casting in Basque cinema, understood as one of the most interesting markers of the continuity of a cinematic production often submerged inside its neighboring cultures. Olivella argues how the iconic value of a given role is reincorporated or alluded to in ulterior productions to (de)construct a sense of cultural identity and/or to question the normative role of masculinity inside Basque society. The paper follows the trajectory of Patxi Bisquert, Karra Elejalde and Xabier Elorriaga as they encompass a shifting masculine subject that is visually recreated in order to sustain or subvert a number of cultural figurations that are central to the Basque imaginary. In the case of Patxi Bisquert, for instance, the narrative persona produced by his lead role in Montxo Armendáriz's *Tasio,* added to his biographical connection to radical forms of political fight, has created an iconic figure strongly related to the Basque conflation of individual resistance and natural resilience. In the case of Karra Elejalde, we are faced with an almost opposite cultural construct, namely, the shifting subject whose masculinity is both vulnerable and excessive in ways that represent the symbolic fissures in the traditional Basque family metaphor. Finally, with the analysis of Xabier Elorriaga's (early) cinematic career, this paper will reveal a form of uncanny identity which is also central to the Basque cinematic production —namely, the figuration of the inner migrant which runs parallel to the very migrancy of Basque cinema itself.

Last but not least, Elena Valdez will take us from the Basque context to Latin America, rethinking Iberian masculinities through different models of being a man in the Dominican Republic. In recent years, the ways of conceptualizing masculinity in the Dominican Republic have undergone a significant shift due to multiple changes in the political situation and to the growth of tourist industry. In her study, Valdez addresses the principal models of Dominican masculinity embodied in the *tíguere*, a male military figure, and a *sanky-panky*. With the notions of masculinity, queerness, and sex tourism theorized by several gender scholars, she will explore how these models are interconnected and transfigured in the twentieth and twenty-first centuries. Furthermore, Valdez will show how contemporary Dominican fiction can shed light on the complex dynamics of constructing these images of masculinity, producing male protagonists who are submerged into the underground world of marginalized queer characters.

Notes

1   Indeed, this collection includes a selection of papers that were originally presented during the "Beyond Don Juan: Rethinking Iberian Masculinities" International Congress, which was held at the Catalan Center at New York University from 30 March through 1 April, 2011. My thanks to the then Director of the Catalan Center and co-organizer of the Congress, Mary Ann Newman, for helping me see the interest, as well as the necessity, of revisiting Iberian masculinities from the national(ist) "peripheries," in general, and from a Catalan perspective, in particular.

2   On Spanish machismo, particularly in Andalusian culture, see, for instance, Gilmore, *Manhood*, 30-55. On machismo in Latin American cultures, see Gutmann, *The Meanings of Macho;* Gonzalez, *Muy Macho*; Mirande, *Hombres y Machos.*

3   See, for example, Blackmore and Hutcheson, *Queer Iberia*; Smith, *Laws of Desire*; Epps and Kakoudaki, *All About Almodóvar*; Mira, *De Sodoma a Chueca*; Fouz-Hernández and Martínez-Expósito, *Live Flesh.*

Bibliography

Blackmore, Josiah and Gregory S. Hutcheson, eds. *Queer Iberia: Sexualities, Cultures, and Crossings from the Middle Ages to the Renaissance.* Durham: Duke University Press, 1999.

Epps, Brad and Despina Kakoudaki, eds. *All About Almodóvar: A Passion for Cinema.* Minneapolis: University of Minnesota Press, 2009.

Fouz-Hernández, Santiago and Alfredo Martínez-Expósito. *Live Flesh: The Male Body in Contemporary Spanish Cinema.* London: I.B. Tauris, 2007.

Gilmore, David. *Manhood in the Making: Cultural Concepts of Masculinity.* New Haven: Yale University Press, 1990.

Gonzalez, Ray. *Muy Macho: Latino Men Confront Their Manhood.* New York: Anchor, 1996.

Gutmann, Matthew. *The Meanings of Macho: Being a Man in Mexico City.* Berkeley: University of California Press, 2006.

Mira, Alberto. *De Sodoma a Chueca: Una historia cultural de la homosexualidad en España en el siglo XX.* Madrid: Egalés, 2004.

Mirande, Alfredo. *Hombres y Machos: Masculinity and Latino Culture.* Boulder: Westview Press, 1997.

Smith, Paul Julian. *Laws of Desire: Questions of Homosexuality in Spanish Writing and Film, 1960-1990.* Oxford: Oxford University Press, 1992.

CHAPTER 1
Saint Sebastian and the Cult of the Flesh: The Making of a Queer Saint in Early Modern Spain

José Cartagena-Calderón
Pomona College

"Let us agree that one of man's most beautiful postures is that of Saint Sebastian."[1] So wrote the Spanish gay poet Federico García Lorca in 1932 on the visual representations of the legendary third-century Roman soldier, who was bound to a stake and shot with the arrows for his efforts to convert other soldiers to Christianity.[2] Penetration, bondage, passivity, sensuality and physical beauty are the salient iconographical features that are conventionally attributed to Saint Sebastian in sacred art since the Renaissance. As a result, during the early modern period the Christian martyr became the ideal source for artists to paint, draw, engrave or sculpture religious, yet deeply homoerotic, works of the male form. These Renaissance and Baroque renditions of the well-known saint have subsequently seduced generations of artists and writers with a queer sensibility, decisively contributing to his undisputable place in today's culture as a virtual poster boy, transcending centuries, for notions of queerness, male beauty and same-sex eroticism. The queering of Saint Sebastian in the visual arts and literature with an emphasis in pre- and early modern Spain will be the focus of this chapter.[3]

There are few saints who exerted such a powerful hold over the artistic imagination of early modern European painters and sculptors as Saint Sebastian. His martyrdom became a favorite subject of some of the greatest Renaissance and Baroque artists, such as Michelangelo, Reni, Bernini, and Bazzi ("Il Sodoma") from Italy and El Greco, Berruguete, Murillo, and Ribera from Spain, to name but a prominent few.[4] Generally depicted as an attractive, nearly naked youth tied to a stake and riddled with arrows, Saint Sebastian is, after Jesus, the most popular and easily recognizable male nude in Catholic iconography. Furthermore, no saint has been more easily associated with the erotic allure of the male body than Sebastian. Whether due to the frequent nudity of his images in paintings, the prevalence of life-like sculptures of his flawless body or the fact that the phallic arrows that penetrate his youthful flesh draw attention to his opulent physique as an epitome of male beauty, Saint Sebastian has transcended mere religious iconography to become an icon of male sexuality and homoeroticism. In the words of art historian Jason Goldman, "Sebastian's supple, near-naked body; the wink-wink symbolism of the penetrating arrows; his thrown-back head expressing a mixture of pleasure and pain; and his inviting gaze all readily contribute to his homoerotic appeal."[5]

St. Sebastian's Carnal Attraction and Its Queer Implications

In an insightful essay on Saint Sebastian's imagery in contemporary culture, Richard Kaye discerns the various incarnations that the martyr has undergone throughout history from a "Christian saint invoked against illness [the plague] in medieval times, exquisite, beardless youth of Apollonian beauty in the Renaissance, 'decadent' androgyne throughout the nineteenth-century, and self-consciously homosexual emblem in the twentieth."[6] Indeed, in contemporary popular culture Saint Sebastian has been removed from its original Christian context and his image has been explicitly appropriated as a homoerotically charged object of desire. The appropriation has been so complete that few modern-day gay men are unfamiliar with the sexualized saint. In paintings, sculptures, photographs, music, videos, films, theater, performance art, literature, and magazine covers, Saint Sebastian has become an archetypal homoerotic figure, enjoying an undeniable presence in queer artistic production.[7] Take, for instance, Yukio Mishima's *Confessions of a Mask* (1948), a work that scandalized Japan for its candid exploration of male same-sex desire. In this semi-autobiographical novel, the adolescent protagonist masturbates over a photograph of a seventeenth-century painting by the Italian artist Guido Reni (fig. 1), which depicts Saint Sebastian in a pose that appears as highly sensual today as it must have seemed to an early modern viewer. Not insignificantly, this is the same image that Oscar Wilde, Ireland's most celebrated gay writer, had found profoundly alluring more than half a century earlier.[8] Mishima himself identified with Reni's depiction, posing as Saint Sebastian in a celebrated 1966 photograph a few years before his 1970 suicide.[9] More striking still, is an all-male feature-length film, entitled *Sebastiane* (1976), directed by the late British filmmaker and gay activist Derek Jarman, which caused considerable controversy for its unabashed homoeroticism and so-called "pornographic" treatment of the saint's legend. The film included men kissing, nude wrestling and erect penises, decisively cementing the saint's status as an archetypal homoerotic figure.[10]

Kaye, a specialist in Victorian literature and culture, has traced the chronologically different meanings projected on Saint Sebastian, elucidating how this meaning changed as gay identities and realities were differently constructed and perceived since the late nineteenth century when the Christian martyr became something of a cult figure for homosexual writers and artists. Mostly focusing on Britain and the United States, Kaye argues that the "history of St. Sebastian as a signifier of male victimhood, masculine beauty, homoerotic desire, and sado-masochistic display is long and intricate," asserting that the symbolic importance of the Christian martyr in the queer imagination became more significant in the late 1980's and 1990's when Sebastian was associated with the AIDS pandemic, which disproportionally struck gay men.[11] The link between the Christian martyr and AIDS may be explained by Sebastian's long-standing resonance in queer culture and his previous role as the patron saint of sufferers of the plague in the Middle Ages. Deeply embedded in the popular imagination in pre-modern Europe was the image of an angry God unleashing the plague epidemic upon the world as an archer unleashes a storm of arrows to all sinners. Since Saint Sebastian was able to survive his first martyrdom by arrows, he was thought to be able to protect his devotees against the "arrows" of the plague. Considered in this light, we can understand why so many altars, chapels and devotional images were commissioned and created in his honor in Medieval and Renaissance Europe, when numerous outbreaks of the dreaded disease ravaged its population with varying intensity.[12] Given our relatively recent experience with cultural responses to AIDS, it should be no surprise that, similar to what happened in the twentieth century with the spread of this devastating disease, when trying to explain the causes of the plague as a social calamity during the pre- and early modern period old prejudices were revived, including the prevalent homophobic idea that the plague was punishment for sodomy.[13]

A particularly compelling example of the way in which Saint Sebastian's image has become relevant in the context of AIDS as the "plague of the Millennium" is a painting entitled *In Memory of all My Dear Friends Who Sacrificed Their Lives Taking Early HIV Medications* by Armando Adrián López (fig. 2). A Mexican-born artist, currently living in New Mexico, López reinterprets Saint Sebastian as an AIDS patient suffering under painfully invasive modern health-care procedures. Reminiscent of Saint Sebastian who was pierced with arrows like a pincushion, this new martyr is punctured by numerous acupuncture needles and hypodermic syringes while receiving fluids from an intravenous drip and holding a glass with a drug cocktail for the treatment of AIDS. The painting invites us to consider the suffering of AIDS patients during the early years of experimentation by the medical establishment as well as the political and ideological implications of Saint Sebastian's deployment in contemporary art.

It is worth noting that although one may think that, as patron saint of plague sufferers, Saint Sebastian would have inspired new religious devotion in the age of AIDS, his place in contemporary gay culture seems more to be as an emblem of queer desire and as a potent symbol of social/political martyrdom than as an object of religious veneration.[14] But exactly when and how Saint Sebastian became a symbol of same-sex eroticism in art and literature and, in Kaye's words, "a touchstone of distinctly homosexual implications" is an intriguing question that has been raised by scholars who are interested in exploring the intersection of homoeroticism and the sacred, as well as the broader implications of this interrelation for the history of sexuality, masculinity and non-normative configurations of desire.[15] Sharing the opinion of respected art historians, such as James Saslow, Dominique Fernandez and Germaine Greer, to name a few, Goldman contends that "Renaissance representations of Saint Sebastianmostly—paintings of a tender, loin-clothed youth writhing in the ecstasy of the arrows that pierce him—are perhaps ground zero for his appointment as the patron saint of gay sensuality."[16] Indeed, there is textual and pictorial support that suggests that Saint Sebastian's representation in literature and visual culture fostered homoerotic implications in the early modern period. For instance, Kaye, among others, argues that "the archetypal Renaissance image of the saint as ecstatically receptive to arrows suggests…a desire for penetration and thus embraces associations of male homosexuality."[17] As we shall see, the homoerotic connotations of a semi-nude young man, tied to a tree trunk, submissively surrendering to his arrow-ridden fate, might not have been completely lost upon male viewers in the early modern period, who were susceptible to falling under the spell of such images of Sebastian's erotic martyrdom.[18]

St. Sebastian's Extreme Makeover: From Byzantine Daddy to Renaissance Twink

Interestingly, when artists first represented Saint Sebastian, his image was neither particularly erotized, nor was he depicted displaying an awe-inspiring, semi-nude young body. One of the earliest representations of the immensely popular martyr in art is a mosaic erected to him in a church in Rome on occasion of the plague in 682.[19] The image represents the saint as a mature man, with a hoary, bearded look, fully dressed in Byzantine court attire while holding the crown of martyrdom. This seventh-century mosaic contains no trace of an arrow. The familiar image of Saint Sebastian as a clean-shaven, nearly naked, attractive youth shot with arrows seems to be a novelty of the Renaissance, when his body was gradually undressed and made younger. Also interesting in this regard is that few early modern artists show the actual death of Saint Sebastian, who, after surviving his first attempted martyrdom by being shot by multiple arrows and recovering from his wounds, was clubbed to death and thrown into a sewer in Rome. One of these artists was the Italian painter Ludovico Carracci, who in a 1612 painting, now housed in the Getty Museum in Los Angeles, depicted Sebastian's beaten body being tossed by soldiers into a cesspit.[20] As journalist Charles Darwent lightheartedly wrote on February 10th of 2008 for the British national morning newspaper, *The Independent*, "had history been less kind, he might have ended up as patron saint of poo."[21]

In striking contrast to earlier images of Saint Sebastian, during the Renaissance the revered martyr experienced what I would call an "extreme makeover," somewhat reminiscent of the many men and women in the popular television program from ABC, who volunteer to receive an extensive makeover in Hollywood, involving plastic surgery, exercise regimens, hairdressing and a new wardrobe. In effect, from the Renaissance on, in image after image, the saint's scruffy beard, grey hair and wrinkles disappeared and his newly acquired young body became softly muscular, miraculously metamorphosizing into a baby-faced Adonis that draws others towards his beautiful self. In fact, most portraits of the saint, such as those painted by nearly all the major artists of the early modern period, build up their composition out of a few main elements: a handsome young man (frequently shown with curly hair), looking good in a loincloth, is shown tied by his hands to a tree or column, while his toned body is pierced by arrows which seem to be caressing rather than violently penetrating his sensuously exposed flesh. The arrows, erotic and phallic symbols, call attention to his stripped youthful carnality, while his eyes, looking upward towards the heavens or rolling back in ecstasy render him as if he were taking orgasmic delight in his suffering. As Maria Wyke pertinently describes Sebastian's iconography: "Nonchalantly posed, nude, fragile, and alone, bound to his post and delicately pierced by a few arrows, his uplifted face is transfixed by an ecstasy that speaks of loss of self, erotic abandon, the *desire* to be penetrated."[22]

St. Sebastian's Erotic Loincloth

Whether Saint Sebastian was portrayed as a delicate, effeminate or androgynous adolescent or as an athletic, muscular, sturdy youth, embodying various forms of masculinity, his nearly naked body became a paragon of male beauty, available to the homoerotic gaze. Moreover, as the Renaissance progressed, painters repeatedly depicted the hunky saint with fewer arrows piercing his accentuated youthful flesh. Some daring artists created less ambiguous homoerotic images of the saint, such as the 1475 rendition of his martyrdom by the Italian painter Pietro Perugino, in which the only arrow that punctures Sebastian's almost naked body is shown penetrating his behind, while simultaneously drawing attention to his loincloth, tied in a knot at the crotch, along with a noticeable excess of fabric hanging like a well-proportioned penis (fig. 3).

In Christian iconography, the loincloth functioned as a semiotic sign for the sexuality of a male figure. For instance, Leo Steinberg has examined, in his now classic study *The Sexuality of Christ in Renaissance Art and in Modern Oblivion*, the persistent attention to Christ's penis during two centuries of Renaissance art, a practice that went into oblivion after centuries of repression and censorship, as the title of his book clearly indicates and his analysis goes on to explore. The recently deceased art critic and historian studied the imagery of the overtly sexed Christ in hundreds of Renaissance paintings in which several artists depicted Jesus on the cross with the suggestion of an erect penis under the covering of his traditional loincloth while others exaggerated the same piece of fabric into wildly suggestive shapes. Much the same can be said of Saint Sebastian's iconography, as Perugino's renditions of his martyrdom and those of other early modern painters attest.[23]

A particularly compelling image of the erotic loincloth can be found in El Greco's paintings of the Christian martyr. In his various renderings of the theme of Saint Sebastian, the Cretan-born painter, sculptor and architect of the Spanish Renaissance, shows a young man with an elongated and athletic body, prettily stuck with arrows, such as in a painting of a life-size Sebastian that hangs since the late 1570's in the Cathedral of Palencia, Spain (fig.4).

The skimpy drapery that barely conceals the young martyr's pubic hairs, hangs perilously low upon his muscular heaps, threatening to expose with the slightest wardrobe malfunction a tantalizing glimpse of his genitals. Perhaps, unsurprisingly, referring to El Greco's paintings of Saint Sebastian and other of his works that have strong homoerotic qualities, such as his sensual Laocoön (1610-1614), the frequently homophobic twentieth-century American writer, Ernest Hemingway, called the famous painter of the Spanish Renaissance "el rey de los maricones."[24] As Richard G. Mann has indicated, when Hemingway made this statement, he also remarked that El Greco's alleged "homosexuality was the primary source of his great creative energy."[25]

The Homoerotics of Martyrdom: St. Sebastian's Manly Archers

Another erotic cue for the queer gaze from the early modern period comes from the abundant number of paintings that represent the violent scene in which the imperial archers are shooting Saint Sebastian with arrows, merging his imagery with sadomasochistic homoeroticism. Referring to the gendered iconography of the Christian martyr and his execution, Wyke claims that "Saint Sebastian's sagittation" functions in these paintings "as the tacit delineation of a forbidden sexual act" in which "the nude body of Sebastian is regularly configured as, in some sense, feminine: passive, submissive, and receptive to penetration by brute masculine force."[26] A case in point is a fifteenth-century painting attributed to the Italian brothers Antonio and Piero Pollaiuolo, entitled the *Martyrdom of Saint Sebastian*, in which the artists show the Christian martyr wearing a translucent loincloth while highlighting his soft, young body against the older, muscular physique of the menacing archers (fig. 5). Commenting on the homoeroticism of this painting, Margaret Walters has also observed that the activity of the robust archers accentuates the erotic passivity of the feminized saint:

The youthful saint is bound to the high stake, and submits dreamily to the gaze of the spectators, and to the arrows. The tough athletic archers are absorbed in activity, some bending to stretch their bows, other poised to take aim. The saint plays the submissive, Christian and feminine role as against the archers' aggressive maleness; the confrontation will be pleasurable, and violent.[27] Equally interested in the homoerotic nuances of this painting, Richard Leppert notices that:

Male homoerotic desire is repeatedly inscribed in the bodies of his torturers, not least via the man in the lower left center who bends down to load his cross bow and, in the process, extends his well-shaped backside for our viewing pleasure. More important, there is an explicit pleasurable tension between the passive, even languid, Sebastian and the archers whose bodies, muscles bulging, are tensed to their aggressive task. Sebastian waits to be penetrated—deeply: The arrows in the bows are far longer than the visible parts of those already piercing him. The active-passive binary driving the relationship is virtually one of violent courtship.[28]

Predictably, an air of controversy surrounded the representation of Saint Sebastian in the visual arts, particularly during the Catholic Reformation of the sixteenth and seventeenth centuries when religious authorities and moralists tried to root out with uneven success the expression of a slight erotic potential in sacred art.

Scandalous St. Sebastian

Indeed, sexualized depictions of Saint Sebastian did not go unnoticed during the early modern period and were constantly held in check by the watchful eye of the Catholic Church, especially after the Council of Trent (1545-1563), which effectively eliminated all nudity in religious art as well as the creation of images that could potentially arouse an erotic response. With Saint Sebastian most likely in mind, the Italian theologian Lancelletto de' Politi (1454-1553) in 1552 railed against images of male nudity displayed in sacred spaces, with the following remarks: "The most disgusting aspect of this age is the fact that you come across pictures of gross indecency in the greatest churches and chapels that [show] all the bodily shames that nature has concealed, with the effect of arousing not devotion but every lust of the corrupt flesh."[29] But perhaps the most emblematic account of scandalous Sebastian comes from the same period, in the middle of the sixteenth-century, from an anecdote described by Giorgio Vasari (1511-1574), a painter and architect from Tuscany, best remembered now as the first Italian art historian. According to Vasari, an altarpiece in a Florentine church painted by the monk Fra Bartolommeo (1472-1517) representing Saint Sebastian as a Christianized Bacchus caused significant anxiety because of its erotic impact on women parishioners who admitted in the confessional that the nude image of the saint was so beautiful and so lascivious that it prompted them to sin with impure thoughts.[30] Vasari did not comment on the impact the painting may have had on the male gaze. To do so might have been simply too scandalous since it would have implied consideration of the altarpiece's impact on members of the clergy who were frequently associated with same-sex transgressions. As art historian James M. Saslow has justifiably pointed out, it should not surprise us that the anxious clerics removed the erotically charged image of Saint Sebastian away from public viewing to their own private quarters, most likely for their privileged enjoyment.[31] Sharing the same opinion, Bette Talvacchia suggests that the now lost painting of Saint Sebastian, "probably had the same effect on the devout monks, since the panel was in short order sold to a private client."[32]

Preoccupations with the decorum of religious images intensified during the second half of the sixteenth century, culminating with the well-known decree promulgated by the Council of Trent in 1563 banning, though not always effectively, nudity in religious art.[33] Renaissance and Baroque artists continued to justify the depiction of sensually nude male bodies by taking, as their subjects, saints and biblical figures whose life stories contained a scene of nudity, such as Saint Sebastian, Saint Laurence, David, John the Baptist, and Jesus himself. Such realistically portrayed, nearly naked male bodies lent themselves to a homoerotic response, regardless of the intention of the artist. In addition, it should be noted that the queer sexual tastes of some eminent artists who painted and carved Saint Sebastian could hardly be questioned, such as the well-documented examples of Leonardo, Michaelangelo, Caravaggio and Bazzi, who was called "Il Sodoma" for his dissident sexuality and "whose public 'coming out' may have been the first in modern European history."[34] Suffice it to say, images of the Apollo-like Christian martyr were still common after the Council of Trent and its reform of Catholic iconography, understandably creating, as Helmut Puff has noted, a tension between homoerotic attraction and religious devotion.[35]

Another notable example of the controversy surrounding the blatant sensuality of images of Saint Sebastian during the early modern period comes from Spain and was firmly voiced by Francisco Pacheco (1564-1644). Pacheco was the censor of painting for the Spanish Inquisition in his native Seville as well as an accomplished artist. He is also best known as the teacher of Diego Velázquez and his eventual father in law. In his influential treatise *Arte de la pintura*, published after his death in 1649, Pacheco documented particular polemics in early seventeenth-century Spanish art theory, while instructing other artists on the proper manner in which various religious subjects should be portrayed.[36] In discussing how visual representations of Saint Sebastian should be executed with "truth" and "decorum," Pacheco cites the work of the Italian cardinal Cesare Baronio (1538-1607), the foremost ecclesiastical historian of his day. According to Pacheco, in his sixteenth-century revised and republished edition of *Martyrologium romanum* (1586), Baronio reproached painters for portraying Saint Sebastian as a smooth-faced youth when the martyred saint should be painted as an older man with a beard, according to an old image, done in mosaic and conserved in a church in Rome.[37] Thus, in the interest of accuracy and decency, and clearly concerned by Saint Sebastian's dangerous beauty, Pacheco anxiously urged other artists to abandon the common practice of portraying the saint as a sexy ephebe who seduced his devotees with his handsome appearance and insisted that the Roman military leader should be depicted as the bearded middle-aged man that he was said to be during his martyrdom in third-century Rome.

Pacheco himself tried his hand at portraying Saint Sebastian in a manner consistent with his seeming prudishness. He was commissioned to portray the saint in an altarpiece for the Hospital of San Sebastián in Alcalá, near Seville, which he completed in 1616. The painting, which no longer exists (it was destroyed in 1936 during the first months of the Spanish Civil War), showed Saint Sebastian being nursed to health by the widow Irene, the saintly woman who, according to the legend, found the martyr alive when he was left all alone in a field by his executioners.[38] In keeping with his Tridentine admonishments, Pacheco's Saint Sebastian is a convalescent middle-aged man with a beard, showing some wrinkles in his drawn face while seating in a bed holding a cup and a spoon. The unappealing, sickly-looking saint is fully clothed, in accordance with the guidelines laid down by the Council of Trent and its efforts to dissuade artists from any lasciviousness in their representations of saints and other devotional images, a decree that Pacheco himself was supposed to enforce in Spain. Needless to say, Pacheco's Counter-Reformation iconographical model of an old and ailing Saint Sebastian who is entirely dressed and holding a cup of soup in bed did not have any followers. Artists both in Spain, across Europe and in Colonial Latin America almost invariably chose to paint Saint Sebastian as a young man with a pagan beauty, who seems unharmed (and sometimes in delight) by the phallic arrows that penetrate his nearly nude body, despite the anxiety towards, and perhaps, recognition of, the latent homoeroticism that such depictions mask.[39]

The Counter Reformation decree on religious art was responsible, however, for the widespread representation of Saint Sebastian portrayals as he is nursed by Irene, often accompanied by angels. This scene was meant (like Pacheco's Saint Sebastian) to emphasize an act of charity performed by a merciful and motherly woman and, within the context of Counter-Reformation goals, to circulate images with a strictly moral and religious message. As Robert Mills has indicated, "the themes of Irene's tender ministrations of the martyr's succoring by angels dominated seventeenth-century treatments of the subject, suggesting that the anxiety over sexualized (or even homosexualized) imagery was the subtext behind much Counter-Reformation polemic."[40] Mills persuasively proposes that the censorship of Saint Sebastian's images could have "stemmed in part from a consciousness of the gender-troubling implications and queer wishes that such paintings aroused."[41]

St. Sebastian's Queer Hagiography

According to the *Legenda aurea* (1275), a rich collection of hagiographies compiled in the thirteenth century by Jacobus da Voragine, a bishop of Genoa who popularized the stories of the Church's saints and whose work was translated into most European languages, Sebastian lived during the third century A.D. at a time when the persecution of Christians intensified as the Roman emperors sought to instill greater loyalty among their people.[42] Legend tells that Sebastian left his birthplace in Gaul, now modern France, and traveled to Italy where he later joined the Roman army, not because he wanted to follow a military life, but because he intended to help persecuted Christians without arousing too much suspicion. The dual Roman emperors Maximian and Diocletian developed a strong affection for Sebastian that prompted them to name him commander of a unit of archers in the elite Praetorian troop while at the same time having him serve as their bodyguard. Sebastian, who was significantly unmarried, came out of the Christian closet when, during the reign of Diocletian, he encouraged two of his military companions who were being tortured for their Christian beliefs to die rather than abandon their faith. When Diocletian learned about this subversive incident, he reproached Sebastian with ingratitude and urged him to renounce his faith and to return to the worship of pagan gods. After refusing the emperor's request, Diocletian furiously ordered his former favorite executed by a squad of archers. He was stripped naked, tied to a stake and shot with so many arrows that he appeared to be a "hedgehog" or a pincushion.

But the martyrdom of Saint Sebastian does not conclude with the story of his dead body peppered by arrows. Instead, the legend continues. Sebastian miraculously survived his bodily torture and Irene, a Christian widow, found him in the Roman field where he was left for dead. After she nursed him back to health, Irene advised Sebastian to leave Rome, but knowing that this was not a time to go into hiding, and with a renewed faith, he returned to the imperial palace where he denounced Diocletian for his violent persecution of Christians. When Sebastian failed to convince the emperor, despite his apparent return from the dead, he was sentenced to death again. The sentence was carried out successfully this time as he was beaten to death with clubs. At the emperor's order, Sebastian's dead body was thrown into a sewer in Rome in order to deprive him of a Christian burial. In spite all these precautions, a women named Lucina, who was also a Christian, was able to recover his remains and, as instructed by Sebastian in a dream, buried him secretly in the catacombs in the Via Appia. Sebastian died towards the end of the third century and a cult developed around his tomb in the fourth century. During that time a church was built over his relics, the present Basilica di San Sebastiano, which attracted numerous pilgrims throughout the pre-modern era.

It is worth pausing a moment to mention that this church is also the site of a beautiful marble sculpture of Saint Sebastian, which was carved towards 1670 by Antonio Giorgetti, who was a disciple of the famous Italian sculptor Gian Lorenzo Bernini.[43] Commenting on the stimulating beauty of this work of art, Donald L. Boisvest writes:

> It is a strikingly attractive piece of religious art, at once ambivalent and arousing. A young, handsome male figure, half-naked and perfectly proportioned, lies on his side, with one hand covering his chest. Longish, curly hair surrounds a head slightly elevated, reclining on the breastplate and helmet of a Roman military officer. The almost naked body is covered sensuously by a rippling piece of cloth, leaving his sinewy legs and chest exposed, while three golden arrows protrude almost lovingly from his chest, biceps, and thigh. The saint looks as though he were asleep, or just napping after a bout of lovemaking. I was mesmerized. Here I was, standing at the site of Saint Sebastian's burial, totally engrossed by the beautiful yet saintly body represented by the statue. I prayed and lit a candle, kneeling in silent and holy adoration before this translucent image of masculine beauty."[44]

Gioggetti's Saint Sebastian is evocative of Bernini's masterpiece *Ecstasy of St. Teresa*, a work that the renowned artist skillfully sculpted between 1647 and 1652 for the Cornaro Chapel at the church of Santa Maria della Vittoria in Rome.[45] The highly controversial sculpture portrays the Spanish saint experiencing what has been perceived (since at least the seventeenth century) as a physical orgasm while an angel points the arrow of divine love at her. In fact, as David B. Morris rightly suggests in a perceptive study on the way culture shapes our perception of pain, Saint Teresa of Avila may be considered "a female counterpart of Sebastian: arrows, pain, beauty, eroticism, and otherworldly vision again prove inseparable."[46]

Mirroring his erotized iconography, accounts of Saint Sebastian's life circulating in the late Middle Ages and early Renaissance, such as the *Legenda aurea* (frequently used by early modern painters and other artists as inspiration for their works), lend themselves to a queer reading that emphasizes how, motivated by a deep affection towards Sebastian, Diocletian kept his favorite soldier close to him and how such intimate homosocial bond was shattered when Sebastian declared to a gathered crowd of his secret devotion to another male figure named Jesus.[47] After this public confession, a betrayed Diocletian condemned his beloved bodyguard to death by being penetrated by scores of arrows shot by his fellow soldiers. As Kaye asserts:

> The details—based on accounts written centuries after Sebastian's death and therefore largely apocryphal—may have helped form Sebastian's subsequent reputation as a homosexual martyr since his story constitutes a kind of "coming out" tale followed by his survival of an execution that may be read symbolically as a penetration.[48]

In a similar vein, Charles Batson contends that the *Legenda aurea* "proffers a same-sex eros as a ringingly silent marker of the description of the relationship between Diocletian and Sebastian," noting that subsequent accounts modeled on this text become infused with an analogous homoerotic charge, "even as they may denotatively occlude it."[49] These references to the intimate emotional bond between Sebastian and the Roman emperor Diocletian made in medieval hagiographies are not, however, the only sources that may have lend themselves to homoerotic interpretations of the martyred saint during the early modern period.[50] In addition to the covert queerness in his hagiography and the patently sensual iconography, another significant source of Saint Sebastian's homoerotic resonance is found in the imaginative literature of the pre- and early modern period.

The Queering of St. Sebastian in Early Modern Spanish Literature

In early modern Spain, Saint Sebastian was more often than not known through visual representations as well as through devotional hagiographies or *Flos sanctorum*, written after the Council of Trent, such as the ones published by Alonso de Villegas in Toledo (1589) and Pedro de Ribadeneira in Madrid (1599-1610), rather than purely literary works. Given the popularity that religious plays enjoyed during the period, it is not surprising that the Spanish stage was the literary form in which Saint Sebastian figured more prominently. The martyred saint was the subject of at least two extant seventeenth-century *comedias de santos*: *El soldado del cielo, San Sebastián*, by Felipe Godínez (1613) and *El soldado más herido y vivo después de muerto*, by Pedro Estenoz y Lodosa (1666). The saint is also the focus of one *auto sacramental*: *El auto de San Sebastián*, by Antonio Carmona (1617). In line with Saint Sebastian's reputation in the visual arts, some of these dramatic works portray him as a source of erotic desire and visual pleasure. For instance, in the religious play *El soldado más herido y vivo después de muerto*, Estenoz y Lodosa stages a conversation between Sebastian and the widow Irene that touches upon the concept of desire as both spiritual and sexual longing. When Irene takes Sebastian into her arms to remove the arrows that have pierced his flesh, a moment that was represented in numerous seventeenth-century paintings in a highly sensual way, the young widow oddly feels the need to reassure him that she is not sexually attracted to him: "The love I have for you,/is pure, chaste, and untainted/free of those desires/that are so harmful to us."[51] We are left to wonder what prompted Irene to utter these words and more particularly to ponder on those desires that she affirms are so harmful to "us." Irene uses the first person plural pronoun ("que tantos daños *nos* causan"/"that are so harmful to *us*") without any gender marker, a point that cannot be underestimated here since it potentially implies that Sebastian may be a source of masculine desire as well. Sebastian's response to Irene does not address the issue of his capacity to unloose erotic yearnings among both men and women, but he reassures her that, despite her beauty, he is not sexually attracted to her: "But more than for your beauty/I love you because you are a Christian woman/so when I say I love you/ it is with the assurance/that my love for you/is the type of love commanded by God."[52] This idea that Sebastian may inspire, but does not necessarily reciprocate, both male and female desire is confirmed by the *gracioso* Limaco who comments on the martyr's rejection of sexual activity with an overt reference to Sebastian's chastity: "my master does not know/ Cupid, nor his tricks…/I have never seen him falling in love."[53]

Sebastian may not be acquainted with Cupid nor his love tricks, but the martyr's reputation to charm the hearts of those who saw his sensual images in Renaissance and Baroque art linked him iconographically to the Roman god of erotic love and beauty, who was often depicted as a youth completely nude with a bow and an arrow. As Ranier Hagen and Rose Marie Hagen remark in their discussion of Renaissance art, Saint Sebastian "became a kind of Christian Apollo, suggestive of Adonis, the darling of the gods, or even of Cupid with his love arrows."[54] In fact, Cupid himself was often painted with his hands tied to a tree as a form of punishment for causing mischief with his arrows, bringing his iconography closer to that of Saint Sebastian. A major seventeenth-century dramatist, Pedro Calderón de la Barca, who has been called the theological poet of the Counter Reformation and who was the author of numerous mythological and religious plays, did not miss this connection between the god of love and the sensuous saint when in his *auto sacramental* entitled *El año santo en Madrid* (1652) wrote: "Ephebe Saint Sebastian covered with arrows is the Heavenly Cupid for women today."[55] This comment may suggest a nervous (or pleasurable) awareness of the erotic aspects underlying Saint Sebastian's iconography, masking as much homoerotic attraction as it displays heterosexual desire.[56]

Another work in which Saint Sebastian makes his way into the Spanish *comedia*, tacitly confirming the homoerotic overtones of the martyr's visual representations in art, is Luis Vélez de Guevara's *La serrana de la Vera*, composed towards the beginning of the seventeenth century.[57] Deliberately reminiscent of Sebastian's martyrdom, the female protagonist, Gila, is executed at the end of the play when she is tied to a stake and shot through with arrows. Vélez de Guevara portrays Gila as a gender non-conformist *mujer hombruna*, who like the physically enticing images of Saint Sebastian in art, is of unusual beauty. The play makes the association with her execution to that of the Christian martyr utterly clear in a conversation between two female characters, who witness the gruesome punishment of the gender-bending protagonist.[58] When Magdalena says, "Now the archers let loose their arrows, Pascuala," the other female character replies, "She seems like Saint Sebastian."[59] What is significant about this unmistakable connection between the play's central character and Saint Sebastian is that Gila represents, as Matthew Stroud rightly observes, "one of the most overtly homosexual figures in the *comedia*."[60] Indeed, Gila's desire for other women is made quite explicit in the play along with her rejection of men and their sexual advances, who despite or perhaps because of her manly attributes feel attracted to her. Thus, the question of queer desire is central to this play not only because there are various references to Gila's non-normative sexuality, but because other "men are erotically drawn to this masculine figure."[61] The phallic arrows that, like the Christian martyr, pierce Gila's beautiful body are an attempt to assert power over her, transforming this "manly woman into that of the womanish man (St. Sebastian)," to borrow George Mariscal's words.[62] As Sherry Velasco aptly notes, "given that the suggestive and sensual images of Saint Sebastian were circulated openly but prohibited by Francisco Pacheco (official censor of visual images for Seville's Inquisition) just two years after the performance of Vélez's play... the playwright most likely knew what he was doing when he compared Gila with the homoerotic images of the saint."[63]

A little more than a century earlier, Joanot Martorell emerged as another Spanish writer who unequivocally compared the masculine hero of his late fifteenth-century chivalry novel *Tirant lo Blanc* with the figure of Saint Sebastian in a homoerotic context. This Catalan romance, first published in Valencia in 1490, gives, in my estimation, further weight to the idea that Saint Sebastian's role, as an emblem of homoerotic desire in today's culture, owes much to his representation in the pre- and early modern period.[64] Critics have frequently observed that Martorell's literary masterpiece is pungently tinged with sexuality, commenting, for example, that the novel is replete with characters that are constantly giving themselves up to the pleasures of the flesh. Interesting in this respect is the work of Peruvian novelist and Nobel Prize winner, Mario Vargas Llosa, who, in an insightful essay on *Tirant*, describes the Catalan romance in the following way: "The love scenes succeed one another till they constitute an authentic erotic spectacle: sexual parties, fetishism, lesbianism, adultery, threats of rape, symbolic incest, voyeurism, techniques of pimping, erogenous play."[65] It is not, therefore, unreasonable to believe that when at the beginning of the seventeenth century the priest in Cervantes' *Don Quixote* praised *Tirant* and declared it "a treasure of happiness and a wealth of entertainment," he was probably thinking of these sexually titillating scenes.[66] Perhaps noteworthy in this regard is the fact that, after rescuing Martorell's sexually graphic chivalry novel from the infamous bonfire, the not so saintly priest enthusiastically urged his good friend, the barber: "Take him home and read him, and you'll see that everything I have said is true."[67]

Indeed, through its many unabashed sex scenes, which also include cross-dressing and total nudity, *Tirant* enables the circulation of non-normative desire and gender fluidity within a heroic narrative full of sexual and gender transgressions, while constructing a hero who at times does not conform to the archetypical images of masculinity. In what follows, I would like to highlight one particular episode that has not been considered in current discussions of the novel's treatment of non-orthodox sexualities. The episode recounts Tirant's shipwreck in North Africa and, as we shall see, inscribes Martorell's novel with male-to-male eroticism by means of an allusion to Saint Sebastian that is intriguingly uttered not by a Christian, but by a Muslim man.

A scene of female homoeroticism notably precedes the episode under consideration. Near the middle of Martorell's text, the Easy-going Widow (the Viuda Reposada), who has fallen in love with Tirant, deceives the knight by making him think that his princess, Carmesina, has not being faithful to him. To get away with her plan, the Easy-going Widow devises a clever hoax in order to fool Tirant into believing that Carmesina is having sex with her father's Muslim gardener, Lauseta. Spying on Carmesina, with the aid of mirrors, through a small window in a hut near the palace garden, Tirant sees Carmesina stepping out of her bedroom bare-breasted to meet Lauseta, who in reality is Pleasure-of-my-life (Plaerdemavida), a lady-in-waiting ingeniously disguised as the black gardener. The Easy-going Widow had a mask made with black leather designed to resemble Lauseta's face and had earlier instructed Pleasure-of-my-life to wear the mask while kissing Carmesina and fondling her breasts and thighs. Scarcely surprising, Pleasure-of-my-life does so with *gusto* (in accordance with her name), giving a spectacular cross-race, cross-class and cross-gender performance. The scene, which, unlike the readers, Tirant thinks is a heterosexual encounter, disheartens him profoundly, since he is persuaded that Pleasure-of-my-life is the male gardener Lauseta. A little later, Tirant manages to capture the real and blameless black gardener and decapitates him. After this violent revenge, Tirant decides to distance himself from Carmesina and goes out into the sea to serve her father in battle, the emperor of Constantinople.

Soon afterward, Pleasure-of-my-life confesses to Tirant the truth about what he had witnessed earlier. However, it is already too late for him to turn back from his ship, which is subsequently driven by a storm to the shores of Barbary, where it is wrecked. The North coast of Africa, a geography reputed in the medieval and early modern imagination for its sexual perversions, including sodomy, becomes the place where the Christian knight momentarily undergoes a peculiar reversal from a position of power as voyeur to a position of subordination or passivity in his subjection to the lustful gaze of non-Christian others.[68] As Vincent Barletta suggests, "It is here that the tables are turned on Tirant: although he had shortly before spied secretly upon Carmesina in the garden near the cottage, it is now his body that serves as an object of inspection by various sets of Muslim eyes."[69] Summarizing what happens next in the episode, Barletta writes:

> As Tirant's men swim to shore from the wreckage, they are captured by a group of Muslims, who kill many of them with their swords. Tirant and a companion manage to reach the shore alive and sleep through the night in a cave situated next to a vineyard. A Muslim hunter chases a hare into the cave and finds the wounded knight sleeping there.[70]

This incident is followed by a scene in which the hunter describes to his superior, the ambassador for the king of Tlemcen in Tunis, what he had accidently witnessed upon entering the cave:

> "Sir, I do not believe that nature can form a human body more perfect, or that a painter can paint one more handsome, than the one that I have seen. Oh fortune, why have you injured him so? I don't know if I saw him properly, but he was so pale that he seemed more dead than alive. Yet his face was remarkably handsome and his eyes had the luster of clear rubies. I cannot believe there is another mortal body in the whole world with such perfect limbs, though I think he is greatly distressed by pain and injury."[71]

Describing Tirant as a sleeping beauty inside a cave, the Muslim hunter acknowledges that the Christian warrior's mesmerizing beauty competes with the attractiveness of the male and female nudes in Medieval and Renaissance paintings. Moreover, the Muslim huntsman praises Tirant's superlative physique using descriptions of female beauty supplied by Petrarch: his stunning face is pale and his eyes sparkle like rubies. The homoerotic undertones of this scene are reinforced when the ambassador himself confesses to Tirant why he felt compassion for him: "I saw you naked, without a shirt, and could clearly observe that your well proportioned body looked like that of the martyred St. Sebastian."[72] Thus, in this significant, but rarely discussed scene Martorell seems to be drawing on the homoerotic aspects inherent in the Christian martyr's iconography while associating the sexually charged gazing with the Muslim Other.

In effect, given the multiple ways in which medieval and early modern Iberian Christian discourses associated Muslims with same-sex erotics, Tirant's naked body becomes the spectacle of the Moors' homoerotically charged gazing, an activity that temporarily unmans the Christian knight. As Mills observes in relation to images of male martyrs in the Middle Ages, although the conflation of nakedness with unmanliness can surely be interrogated, nudity may signal "the intervention of the gaze of others, with all the potential objectification and de-virilization that that implies."[73] Not insignificantly, Tirant is first viewed as an object of same-sex desire by a Muslim in a scene of hunting, an activity highly suggestive of erotic symbolism, and inside a cave, a symbol associated with the feminine, but also, like the distinctly erotic arrow imagery, with the act of penetrating. This homoerotic scene is followed by another queer moment in which Tirant's naked body is compared with Saint Sebastian, who in Martorell's time emerged as an extraordinarily popular subject for painters and was frequently depicted, as discussed earlier, with strong homoerotic undertones. Consequently, Martorell could have hardly made clearer the connection between his Christian hero's homoerotic allure and that of the famously penetrated saint.

What is striking about the explicit parallel between Tirant and Saint Sebastian is that the erotized and exhibited flesh of both Christian figures is pointedly portrayed as being objectified by the Muslim Other. In early modern paintings and drawings the enticing body of Saint Sebastian is occasionally shown being penetrated by suggestive phallic arrows that are shot by archers who are often depicted as dark-skinned males wearing a turban and sporting a beard, an image that functioned as a powerful ethnic or racial marker of Muslim identity. This tendency found artistic expression in a painting of the saint's martyrdom created in 1469 as part of an altarpiece placed in the Augustinian nuns' convent of Rubielos de Mora, in the region of Aragon (fig. 6). The "Altarpiece of the Epiphany," as it is called, is now housed at the Museu Nacional d'Art de Catalunya in Barcelona and was painted by Joan Reixach, who was active in Valencia during the second half of the fifteenth century, a period that coincides with *Tirant*'s date and place of publication in 1490.[74]

It should be noted that the portrayal of Saint Sebastian's archers as Muslims is in keeping with other cultural products of the same period. For instance, in his study on the *morismas*, the popular festivals of mock battles between Moors and Christians from medieval and early modern Spain, as well as from Colonial Mexico, Max Harris has commented on the curious fact that representations of Saint Sebastian's tormentors as Muslims or Turks were given copious expression.[75] This was the case in fifteenth century Catalonia, where the *morismas* used to be enthusiastically performed, a moment and place in time that, like Reixach's painting, corresponds with the appearance of Martorell's text.

The depiction of the martyr's masculine penetrators as Muslims is an intriguing detail since, as Harris reminds us, Saint Sebastian is believed to have been martyred in Rome, towards the end of the third century, "long before the birth of Muhammad or the Spanish conflict with Islam."[76] Furthermore, the foundational hagiography of Saint Sebastian and main source of his legend, the *Passio S. Sebastiani*, written two centuries after his martyrdom by an unknown author, does not make any mention of the race or ethnicity of the archers.[77] Not insignificantly, other hagiographical sources that circulated in Spain during the period, such as the *Flos sanctorum* compiled by Pedro de Ribadeneyra or the one prepared by Alonso de Villegas, are equally silent about the archers' ethnicity. This fact points strongly to the idea that the Muslim bowmen were an anachronistic link that Christian artists established between Saint Sebastian and Islam in the pre- and early modern era. As Mills contends, in the medieval and early modern period "martyrdom iconography, after all, frequently relates the struggle between Christianity and the pagan 'other' by assimilating current constructions of heretics, Jews and Muslims with the fictional tormentors (all which might be coupled with aberrant sexuality [or] sodomy)."[78] In effect, we only need to think of the well-known legend of Saint Pelagius of Cordova, a Christian boy who in the tenth century prefers to be martyred rather than give in to the sexual advances of a Muslim caliph.[79] For centuries, the cult of Saint Pelagius is thought to have imparted a strong spiritual impetus for the Iberian *Reconquista*, largely because it condemned the so-called sodomitic vices of the Muslim enemies. To borrow again Mills' words, "Pelagius is clearly cast as a figure who heroically confronts a troubling form of desire (which, in a typical conjunction of racist ideology with homophobia, is constituted as alien to the Christian world)."[80]

The significance underlying the not infrequently cultural, religious and artistic representation of Saint Sebastian's bowmen as distinctly Muslim men cannot be overlooked. The Renaissance pictorial treatment of the youthful saint's carnality being symbolically penetrated by older, hyper-masculine looking men (without necessarily identifying their race or ethnicity) is, in and on itself, a potent image that could have aroused a homoerotic response among some early modern viewers, however unintentional. The artistic works that portrayed the aggressively "penetrating" pagan executioners as Muslims may be understood as yet another way in which Saint Sebastian was queered in a very distant past. This particular way of seeing is strongly reinforced by the fact that hegemonic cultural discourses that circulated during the medieval and early modern period consistently racialized sodomy by claiming that it was a dominant practice among Turks and Moors. Thus, there is plenty of room for arguments that suggest such cultural and religious images could have potentially expressed, invoked or mobilized possibilities of male-to-male desire, while simultaneously exorcising them by displacing them onto non-Christians others. Notwithstanding this common strategy of containment, such stirring up of homoerotic possibilities through the figure of Saint Sebastian and the "sodomitic Moor" provided, I would argue, yet another cultural space in which early modern Spaniards could have experienced queer modes of looking, reading and imagining.

Figure 1. Guido Reni, "St. Sebastian" (ca. 1615), Palazzo dei Conservatori, Pinacoteca Capitolina. Photo: Wikimedia Commons.

Figure 2. Armando Adrián-López, "In Memory of All My Dear Friends Who Sacrificed Their Lives Taking Early HIV Medications" (2006). Reprinted by kind permission of the artist. All rights reserved.

Figure 3. Pietro Perugino, "Saint Sebastian" (ca. ca. 1489-90), Stockholm, National Museum. Photo: Wikimedia Commons.

Figure 4. El Greco, "Saint Sebastian," (ca. 1577-1578),
Cathedral Sacristy, Palencia, Spain. Photo: Wikimedia Commons.

Figure 5. Antonio and Piero Pollaiuolo, "Martyrdom of Saint Sebastian"
(ca. 1473-1475), The National Gallery, London.
Photo: Wikimedia Commons.

Figure 6. Joan Reixach, "Altarpiece of the Epiphany" (ca. 1469), Museu Nacional d'Art de Catalunya in Barcelona. Author's photo.

Notes

1   García Lorca, *Poet in New York*, 186.

2   Given Sebastian's homoerotic depictions in visual culture, it should not amaze anyone that Lorca's fascination with the saint was inextricably interwoven with his complex, rumored-to-be romantic relationship to the Catalan painter Salvador Dalí. The two influential artists were particularly drawn to the popular saint, which they each represented in writings and drawings. Taken as a whole, their correspondence suggests an awareness of the homoerotic aspects underlying the artistic representations of the martyred Christian saint. For a discussion of Saint Sebastian's treatment in Lorca's and Dalí's *oeuvre*, see Christopher Maurer's "Prologue" of his edition and English translation of a selection of letters, texts, and images by both artists, suggestively entitled *Sebastian's Arrows: Letters and Mementos of Salvador Dalí and Federico García Lorca*. For a nuanced consideration of the relationship between constructions of masculinity and homoerotic desire in relation to Lorca's engagement with visual representations of Saint Sebastian in his plays, see José I. Badenes, "Martyred Masculinities."

3   It must be emphasized from the outset that in this chapter I use the notoriously slippery term "queer" to designate cultural practices of eroticism that resist, are at odds with, or call into question the very category of the "normal," the "conventional" or the "natural." By "queering" I mean not only the representation of homoeroticism by writers and artists, but also the current scholarly endeavor to recuperate non-normative evocations of erotic desire in visual and literary texts from a distant past. A guiding assumption of my analysis of the queering of Saint Sebastian in the period under consideration is that, similar to other outlets of artistic expression (such as imaginative literature), pre-modern Christian iconography is not devoid of erotic, let alone homoerotic content. For a useful discussion of the deployment of the term "queer" in academic circles and in the culture at large, see Noreen Giffney and Michael O'Rourke, *The Ashgate Research Companion to Queer Theory*. For an astute and illuminating study of the highly charged homoerotic imagery that permeates religious devotional art and literature since the early modern period, see Richard Rambuss, *Closet Devotions*. Focusing on Anglo-Saxon Christian literary and cultural production of the seventeenth century, Rambuss details how religious experience was indeed expressed, imagined and experienced (homo)erotically. In simpler terms, his study examines how religious devotion and (homo)erotic desire were inextricably intertwined.

4   Irving L. Zupnick ("Saint Sebastian," 242-243), makes the useful point that, in addition to being invoked against the plague as early as the seventh century, "there were many reasons for artists to depict Saint Sebastian. He was the patron saint of cities such as Rome and Milan, or Soissons, where Bishop Hilduin brought his relics in 826. His relics are preserved at Mantua, Malaga, Seville, Toulouse, Munich, Paris, Tournai, Antwerp and Brussels. He was also the patron saint of crusaders, lace-makers, crossbowmen and archers, of arquebusiers, iron merchants, and oddly, of hose-makers in France (whose punning slogan was 'Ses bas se tiennent.'" Because the arrows that pierce his body resemble pins in a cushion, Sebastian additionally became the patron saint of pinmakers. Sebastian is also considered the patron saint of athletes and soldiers, making him the patron saint of a "certain type" of male bonding.

5   Goldman, "Subject of the Visual Arts," 322.

6   Kaye, "Losing His Religion," 87.

[7] For a useful collection of essays and pictorial material on Saint Sebastian as an enduring homoerotic icon, see Gerald Matt and Wolfgang Fetz's *Saint Sebastian: A Splendid Readiness for Death*. Most images of Saint Sebastian mentioned in this chapter may be conveniently accessed via http://bode.diee.unica.it/~giua/SEBASTIAN/ Entitled "The Iconography of Saint Sebastian," the website is divided into three main sections: (1) paintings; (2) sculpture; and (3) drawings, photographs and other techniques. This digital archive includes countless images of the Christian martyr from various periods and countries and is updated regularly.

[8] Guido Reni was the painter *par excellence* of Saint Sebastian, leaving several surviving versions of his martyrdom. Renaissance paintings and other visual representations of the Christian martyr, such as Reni's and Mantegna's renditions, inspired a widespread *fin de siècle* fascination with the penetrated saint in male homosexual circles, which confirms the erotic overtone of his iconography, particularly its homoerotic potential. One prominent example is Oscar Wilde's *Picture of Dorian Gray*, a homoerotically inflected work published in 1890, in which the decadent protagonist wears a cape adorned with a medallion of Saint Sebastian. Wilde, who was about as out of the closet as was possible for the late nineteenth century and who developed a great fondness for Reni's seventeenth-century sensuous painting of the martyr, used the alias "Sebastian Melmoth," which he adopted when he moved to France following his release from a London prison where he served two years on a sodomy charge. For a detailed discussion of Saint Sebastian's homoerotic treatment in Victorian literature and the culture's fascination with Renaissance Italy that fueled interest in the saint, see Kaye, "'Determined Raptures.'"

[9] For a reproduction of the photograph, see Matt and Fetz, *Saint Sebastian: A Splendid Readiness for Death*, 78.

[10] On the regular appropriation and frequent deployment of Saint Sebastian as a homoerotic icon in contemporary Spanish culture, see José Manuel Buján Bran, "Algunos términos."

[11] Kaye, "St. Sebastian: The Uses of Decadence," 11.

[12] The first documented instance of Sebastian's invocation against the plague occurred during the disastrous outbreak in the 680s in Rome. It was said that the city would be spared if an altar were erected to the early Christian martyr in San Pietro in Vicoli. Although the altar no longer exists, the church still contains one of the oldest known images of Saint Sebastian.

[13] In an insightful and necessary study on the history of homophobia from antiquity to the present time, Byrne Fone (*Homophobia: A History*, 6-7) affirms: "Invented, fostered, and supported over time by different agencies of society—religion, government, law, and science—it tends to break out with special venom when people imagine a threat to the security of gender roles, of religious doctrine, or of state and society, or the sexual safety and health of the individual." Additionally, Fone (ibid.) rightly observes that in today's society, "some Christian fundamentalists even insist that homosexuals afflicted with AIDS are sinners appropriately punished by divine retribution." In an early modern context, Michael Rocke (*Forbidden Friendships*, 28) has remarked that in Renaissance Florence, where the disease was particularly virulent, the association of the plague with the practice of sodomy "did not escape contemporaries such as the influential preacher Bernardino of Siena, who made it a major theme of his terrifying sermons against sodomy in Florence and Siena in the mid-1420s," and who "blamed sodomites for causing the plague, which he claimed was God's retribution for their sins."

[14] With this statement I do not mean to imply that Saint Sebastian does not have any significance to gay men inside the Catholic faith nor that Christian gay men have not

reclaimed him as an icon of homoerotic desire. Peter Savastano ("St. Gerard," 181-186) reminds us of the importance of saints to practicing gay Catholics. In particular, he explains that identifying with a saint offers an opportunity for people to "make a place for themselves" within the church, observing that for a practicing Catholic homosexual, certain saints, such as Saint Sebastian, can function as "a symbol with which to navigate the rough waters of being both gay and Catholic." See also Donald L. Boisvert, *Sanctity and Male Desire*.

[15]   Kaye, "Losing His Religion," 88.

[16]   Goldman, "Subject of the Visual Arts," 321. See also Dominique Fernandez, *A Hidden Love*, 90-106, and Germaine Greer, *The Beautiful Boy*, 204-212.

[17]   Kaye, "Losing His Religion," 89.

[18]   Early modern literary critics, particularly of English literature, have brought to light some literary works that support the idea that Saint Sebastian was understood in homoerotic terms in the Renaissance, particularly in the works of William Shakespeare, known for offering its audience and readers a myriad of homoerotic possibilities both in his comedies and love sonnets. According to these critics, in the early modern period the very name Sebastian carried homoerotic connotations, largely because of the martyr's sexualized iconography. For the queering of Saint Sebastian in Elizabethan literature, see Mario DiGangi, *The Homoerotics of Early Modern Drama*, 20.

[19]   For a printed reproduction of this seventh-century mosaic, see Karim Ressouni-Demigneux, *Saint-Sébastien*, 12.

[20]   For an illustration of this painting, see "St. Sebastian Thrown into the Cloaca Maxima (Getty Museum)" http://www.getty.edu/art/gettyguide/artObjectDetails?artobj=690

[21]   Darwent, "Arrows of Desire" http://www.independent.co.uk/artsentertainment/art/features/arrows-of-desire-how-did-st-sebastian-become-an-enduring-homoerotic-icon-779388.html

[22]   Wyke, "Playing Roman Soldiers," 253-254.

[23]   Nigel Jonathan Spivey (*Enduring Creation*, 91) writes that "there are no fewer than eleven known paintings by Pietro Perugino of St. Sebastian and, typically (of such a prolific artist), he more or less recycled his own vision of the saint, invariably languid and hygienic."

[24]   Quoted in Richard Fantina, *Ernest Hemingway: Machismo and Masochism*, 91.

[25]   Mann, "GLBTQ: An Encyclopedia" http://www.glbtq.com/arts/greco_e,2.html

[26]   Wyke, "Playing Roman Soldiers," 253.

[27]   Walters, *The Nude Male*, 114.

[28]   Leppert, *Art and the Committed Eye*, 254-256.

[29]   Quoted in David Freedberg, *The Power of Images*, 239.

[30]   Interestingly, the English edition of *Vasari's Lives of Italian Painters* that I consulted does not specify the gender of the parishioners who were seduced by Fra Bartolommeo's image of Saint Sebastian. Havelock Ellis'edition simply states (144): "It is said that when his painting was put up in the church, the monks discovered, from what they heard in the confessionals, that the grace and beauty of the vivid imitation of life, imparted to his work by the talents of Fra Bartolommeo, had given occasion to the sin of light and evil thoughts; they consequently removed it from the church and placed it in the Chapter House."

[31]   Saslow, *Pictures and Passions*, 99.

[32]   Talvacchia, "The Double Life of St. Sebastian," 246. For a reproduction of a copy of the now believed to be lost painting of Saint Sebastian by Fra Bartolommeo, see Ressouni-

Demigneux, *Saint-Sébastien*, 79 62. The painting reproduced in Ressouni-Demigneux' book was identified in the 1970s by Janet Cox-Rearick at San Francesco in Fiesole and is considered to be a relatively faithful copy of Fra Bartolommeo's lost Saint Sebastian with an Angel. For a detailed analysis of Bartolommeo's painting of Saint Sebastian, see Cox-Rearick, "Fra Bartolomeo's."

[33] In reference to the artistic depiction of saints, the Decrees of the Council of Trent (December 4, 1563) proscribed that "all lasciviousness [must be] avoided, so that images shall not be painted and adorned with a seductive charm." Cited in Henry Joseph Schroeder, *Canons and Decrees of the Council of Trent*, 216. Mary Hollingsworth (*Art in World History*, 280) succinctly sums up the Council of Trent's efforts to establish and implement rules and regulations governing religious art: "In response to the Protestant condemnation of religious images as idolatrous, the Council also attempted to redefine the boundaries between sacred and profane images, which had become blurred in the religious art of the fifteenth century. Recognizing the power of art to influence the human spirit, the Council laid down strict guidelines for both style and content of religious art. Nudity was banned not only for its pagan overtones but also because it was inappropriate and potentially lascivious. Paul IV (1550-1559), who had been appointed the first Inquisitor General by Paul III, had fig leaves added to the Vatican collection of antique sculpture. Daniele da Volterra was commissioned to paint draperies on Michaelangelo's nudes in the *Last Judgment*. Spirituality replaced secularization."

[34] Richard E. Spear, *The "Divine" Guido*, 57. On this topic, Talvacchia ("The Double Life of Saint Sebastian," 240-241) asserts that Saint Sebastian's iconography "permitted Renaissance artist and viewers who preferred male beauty and male sexual partners to find particular resonance in physically enticing images of Sebastian," suggesting that this could be inferred "from our information that among his possessions in 1481, Leonardo da Vinci owned eight images of the saint." Fernandez (*A Hidden Love*, 91) is careful to note that "it would be ridiculous, however, to claim all painted or carved St. Sebastians as evidence of homosexual eroticism."

[35] Puff, "Early Modern Europe," 101.

[36] According to Jonathan Brown (*Painting in Spain*, 102), "this book is the labor of almost four decades; it was started around 1600 and brought to completion by 1638, although the publication was mysteriously delayed for another eleven years."

[37] "Baronio reprehende a los pintores que pintan mancebo a San Sebastián, debiéndole pintar con aspecto y barba de viejo, conforme a la imagen antigua de mosaico que hoy se conserva entera en la iglesia de San Pedro ad vincula, en Roma." In Francisco Pacheco, *Arte de la pintura*, 327.

[38] For a black and white reproduction of Pacheco's painting, see Peter Mitchell, "The Politics of Morbidity," 83.

[39] For a homoerotic reading of a painting representing Saint Sebastian by the Valencian born artist Jusepe de Ribera (1591-1652), who spent most of his years in Rome and Naples, and who, like Reni, did various renditions of the Christian martyr, see Alain Saint-Saëns, "Homoerotic Suffering," 51-57.

[40] Mills, "'Whatever You Do,'" 33.

[41] Ibid.

[42] Wyke ("Playing Roman Soldiers," 248), among others, notes that the legend of Saint Sebastian is without historical foundation: "The martyred body of Saint Sebastian is certainly shrouded in darkness where the historical record is concerned... So meager is the ancient evidence concerning Sebastian that it has led some scholars to question

whether he ever existed... Scholars of the early Church are in general agreement that all subsequent record for Sebastian is entirely unhistorical, for the saint possesses no 'authentic' *Acts*. The initial, foundational hagiographic recital of Saint Sebastian's deeds and death is the anonymous *Passio S, Sebastiani* whose composition is attributed to the period 432-40 C.E."

43   For a fine reproduction of Giorgetti's Saint Sebastian, see Fernandez, *A Hidden Love*, 102.

44   Boisvert, *Sanctity and Male Desire*, 47-48.

45   For an illustration of Bernini's sculpture, see Edward Mornin and Lorna Mornin, *Saints: A Visual Guide*, 254.

46   Morris, *The Culture of Pain*, 131.

47   James Saslow has documented elements of homoeroticism attached to Saint Sebastian since at least the Italian Renaissance, especially in sacred images that portray the Christian martyr with Jesus. According to Saslow ("The Tenderest Lover," 61), "the position of Sebastian" in these paintings "is one among a number of male figures close to Jesus, with its concomitant suggestions of Jesus' general susceptibility to male-male relationships." The homoerotic aspects in early modern visual and textual representation of Jesus and other sacred male figures are beyond the scope of this chapter. For a discussion, with pictorial examples and a useful bibliography, of the ways in which Christ's nude body could have aroused homoerotic responses in a pre-modern context, see Mills, "Ecce Homo." See also, Rambuss, *Closet Devotions*, in particular his discussion of what he appropriately calls a "devotional homoerotics."

48   Kaye, "Sebastian, St," 606.

49   Batson, *Dance, Desire, and Anxiety*, 12.

50   Kaye, *"Losing His Religion,"* 89.

51   "El amor que yo te tengo/es puro, casto, y sin manchas,/sin aquellos deseos,/que tantos daños nos causan." In Estenoz y Lodosa, *El soldado más herido,* fol. 148. In reference to the erotic undertones in the Saint Irene motif in the visual arts, Zupnick ("Saint Sebastian," 257) observes that "generally in depictions of the Saint Irene theme, the wounded Saint Sebastian is unconscious, shifting the major emphasis from the violence and painfulness of his ordeal to the tender and sympathetic ministrations of Saint Irene. Sometimes, as in the painting by Antonio Balestra in the Hermitage, there is something romantic, if not erotic, about the situation, which may explain why the subject was also interesting for nineteenth-century artists like Delacroix." Greer (*The Beautiful Boy*, 208-209) adds another interesting observation regarding this popular theme in the seventeenth century: "Because the female figure could not be seen in too close contact with the boy's naked body, St. Irene is often no more than a head and an arm, gingerly approaching the languishing saint, with none of the two-handed aggression needed actually to extract an embedded arrow from flesh, bone and sinew. Sometimes the problem is solved by presenting Irene as an old woman, with the added benefit that the contrast with her grizzled features makes Sebastian appear yet more beautiful. Another way of solving the problem was to transform Irene into a couple of ministering angels. When these dwindle into cherubs, Sebastian's perforation seems closer to erotic play than ever."

52   Pero más que por hermonsa/te quiero por ser Christiana;/y assí digo, que te quiero,/pero con aquella salva/de quererte, por quererte/en la forma que Dios manda." In Estenoz y Lodosa, *El soldado más herido,* fol. 149.

53   "que mi amo no conoce/a Cupido, ni sus tretas.../Jamás le vi enamorado..." Ibid., fol. 146b.

[54]   Hagen and Hagen, *What Great Paintings Say*, 75.

[55]   "San Sebastián,/ joven de flechas cubierto,/ es hoy para las mujeres,/ el Cupido de los cielos." In Calderón de la Barca, *El año santo en Madrid*, 157.

[56]   It is further worth mentioning that there are other early modern Spanish plays in which an implied linkage between Saint Sebastian and erotic desire appears, albeit in a heterosexual context, as in Lope de Vega's play *El acero de Madrid*, in which the Church of Saint Sebastian (where Lope de Vega's remains were initially buried) is described as an opportune locale for amorous encounters and where, according to the character Belisa, she met and fell in love with Lisardo: "Aquel mancebito/que me vio en la iglesia/de San Sebastián/me tiró mil flechas" (that lad who saw me in the Church of Saint Sebastian shot me with a thousand arrows). In Lope de Vega, *El acero de Madrid*, 116.

[57]   In addition to the *comedias de santos* dedicated to Saint Sebastian in Spain and his occasional references in other early modern plays, of which *La serrana de la Vera* is just one example, there are allusions to the saint's martyrdom in various dramatic works by major seventeenth-century Spanish playwrights such as Lope de Vega, Vélez de Guevara, Francisco de Villegas and Calderón de la Barca. All these center on King Sebastian of Portugal, who was born on January 20, 1554 (on the feast of Saint Sebastian) and died in 1578 fighting the Moors in a quixotic expedition into Northern Africa that left Portugal in a political chaos. During the early modern period, King Sebastian was frequently linked to Saint Sebastian in ways that go beyond their shared Christian name and, just like the martyr's association with non-normative forms of desire, the monarch's own sexuality has been, since the sixteenth century, a longstanding topic of rumors and innuendos. On King Sebastian's rumored homosexuality, see Harold Johnson, "A Padophile in the Palace."

[58]   Vélez de Guevara's Gila participates in what Mills ("Whatever You Do," 15, n. 39) has aptly called "the gender-inverting *topoi* of male martyrdom legends," which in the case of Saint Sebastian, "has been noticed by modern redactors, as exemplified by Gabriele d'Annunzio and Claude Debussy's production of the 'Martyrdom of St. Sebastian' (May 22, 1911), which cast a woman, Ida Rubinstein, in the lead role: it was the scandal of Paris, whose archbishop proclaimed it blasphemous." Commenting on Rubinstein's performance as Saint Sebastian in d'Annunzio's play (who, by the way, happened to be a Jewish lesbian dancer), Wyke ("Playing Roman Soldiers," 255-256), observes that "the apparent perversity of allotting the martyr's role to a woman, of rendering Sebastian a decadent, androgynous icon, may have been exacerbated by the current medicalization of homosexuality as a congenital abnormality, a distinctly feminine illness, which led to a widely circulated definition of the homosexual as *anima muliebris virili corpore inclusa* ('a female mind trapped in a male body')." Kaye ("St. Sebastian: The Uses of Decadence," 14), for his part, has remarked on the numerous female Saint Sebastians in contemporary art, a topic that merits a study of its own, especially in relation to the appropriation of the saint by women artists. Among the prominent examples that Kaye discusses is the Mexican painter Frida Kahlo, "who drew on the imagery of St. Sebastian for several of her works completed in the 1930's and 40's."

[59]   "Ya disparan las saetas/ los cuadrilleros, Pascuala;" "A San Sebastián pareze." In Vélez de Guevara *La serrana de la Vera*, 204.

[60]   Stroud, *Plot Twists*, 140.

[61]   Ibid., 132.

[62]   Mariscal, "Symbolic Capital," 152.

[63]   Velasco, *Lesbians in Early Modern Spain*, 134.

64   For another early modern literary work that invites us to consider Saint Sebastian in association with the subject of same-sex desire, as well as with notions of imperialism and otherness in a trans-Atlantic context, see Ricardo Padrón "Love American Style." In this incisive analysis of Alonso de Ercilla's *La Araucana*, Padrón reveals how the Amerindian hero, Caupolicán, is suggestively linked to the martyred saint at the end of the epic poem, while exploring the ideological and political implications of this curious association.

65   "Los cuadros amorosos se suceden hasta constituir una verdadera exposición erótica: fiestas sensuales, fetichismo, lesbianismo, adulterios, amagos de violaciones, un incesto simbólico, *voyeurisme*, técnicas de alcahuetería, juegos erógenos." In Vargas Llosa, *Carta de batalla*, 20.

66   Cervantes Saavedra, *Don Quixote*, 44.

67   Ibid.

68   Like other European nations, who drew a strong connection between sodomy and foreignness, same-sex erotics in pre- and early modern Spain was consistently associated to national, imperial or ethnic otherness, whether Moor, Turk, Italian, French or Amerindian. There are countless references in fictional texts and non-literary discourses of the period highlighting the characteristic inclination of Moors and Turks towards sodomy and of North Africa as a breeding ground of male same-sex activity. For instance, Cervantes alludes to the stereotyped figure of the sodomitic Turk or Moor in many of his works, including *Don Quixote*, his Algerian plays (one of which has a Christian character, a boy, significantly named Sebastian) and exemplary novels. On this topic, see Adrienne Martín, "Images of Deviance." Additionally, as Carroll Johnson (*Cervantes and the Material World*, 133) reminded us, in the first years of the seventeenth century, Diego de Haedo described how sodomy was openly practiced in Algiers when he lamented in his *Topografía e historia general de Argel* that "they all live a bestial life of porcine animals, giving themselves over constantly to drunkenness and sex, and in particular to stinking and unspeakable sodomy. They use captive Christian boys that they buy just for this purpose and then dress Muslim style, or they use the sons of Jews and Moors from Algiers and other places, taking and keeping them, getting drunk on wine and spirits." Unsurprisingly, the Inquisition commonly accused North Africans of sodomy, as E. William Monter has shown. E. William Monter, *Frontiers of Heresy*, 292.

69   Barletta, *Death in Babylon*, 13. It should be noted here that in his fine analysis of Tirant's episode in North Africa, Barletta does not address the homoeroticism deployed by the explicit comparison between Tirant and Saint Sebastian. Instead, Barletta (ibid., 14) puts a different emphasis on the symbolism of this scene, focusing on how Tirant "is stripped of his clothes, his consciousness, his subjectivity, and his agency upon his arrival in North Africa," and commenting on how the comparison with the saint frames the Christian knight "as a naked object of aesthetic judgment (and interpretation) while liking him to the theme of violent death."

70   Ibid., 13.

71   Martorell, *Tirant lo Blanc*, 580.

72   Ibid., 585.

73   Mills, "'Whatever You Do,'" 13.

74   For further visual and textual examples that depict Saint Sebastian's archers as Muslims from the Middle Ages to the twentieth century, see Buján Bran, "Homoerotismo," 265-271.

[75] Harris, *Aztecs, Moors, and Christians*, 43-53.

[76] Ibid., 44.

[77] The *Acta S. Sebastiani* (1056) only says: "Tunc posuerant eum milites in medio campo et hinc inde eum ita sagittis repleverunt, ut quasi hericius ita esset hirsutus ictibus sagittarum."

[78] Mills, "'Whatever You Do,'" 21.

[79] In *The Passion of Saint Pelagius* (dated 962), Hrotswitha, canoness of the Benedictine monastery of Gandersheim in Saxony, offers what is perhaps one of the earliest Christian writings in which the perceived connection between sodomy and Islam is unambiguously established. In this tenth-century biography of the saint, Hrotswitha recounts the martyrdom in the year 926 of the young Christian prince Pelagius, who was tortured and dismembered for allegedly refusing the sexual advances of Abd ar-Rahman III, Emir and Caliph of Córdoba. For an analysis of the sodomitic episodes in the legend of Saint Pelagius and homoerotic aspects of his iconography, as well as the permutations in the saint's passion in the context of Christian theology, see Mark D. Jordan, "Saint Pelagius." See also, Gregory S. Hutcheson, "The Sodomitic Moor." For a persuasive discussion of the legend of Saint Pelagius *vis à vis* the construction of an idealized Christian masculinity in pre- and early modern Spain based on sexual austerity and the belief that Islamic men consistently and openly engaged in homosexual behavior, see Michael J. Horswell, *Decolonizing the Sodomite,* 29-40.

[80] Mills, "'Whatever You Do,'" 25.

Bibliography

"Acta S. Sebastiani Martyris." In *Patrologiae Latinae. Cursus Completus. Omnium Ss. Patrum, Doctorum Escritorumque Ecclesiasticorum Sive Latinorum, Sive Graecorum. Sancti Ambrossii, Mediolanensis Episcopi*, edited by J. P. Migne. Vol. 16. Turnhout, Belgium: Ed. Turnholti, 1967.

Badenes, José I. "Martyred Masculinities: Saint Sebastian and the Dramas of Tennessee Williams and Federico García Lorca." *Text & Presentation: The Comparative Drama Conference Series* 5, (2008): 5-17.

Barletta, Vincent. *Death in Babylon: Alexander the Great & Iberian Empire in the Muslim Orient*. Chicago: The University of Chicago Press, 2010.

Batson, Charles R. *Dance, Desire, and Anxiety in Early Twentieth-Century French Theater: Playing Identities*. Burlington, VT: Ashgate, 2005.

Boisvert, Donald L. *Sanctity and Male Desire: A Gay Reading of Saints*. Cleveland: Pilgrim Press, 2004.

Brown, Jonathan. *Painting in Spain: 1500-1700*. New Haven: Yale University Press, 1998.

Buján Bran, José Manuel. "Algunos términos para un abecedario homoerótico de la iconografía contemporánea de San Sebastián mártir." In *Miradas sobre la sexualidad en el arte y la literatura del siglo XX en Francia y España*, edited by Juan Vicente Aliaga, Ashmed Haderbache, Ana Monleón and Domingo Pujante. 201-208. Valencia: Universitat de València, 2001.

———. "Homoerotismo en la iconografía de San Sebastián mártir. Una visión desde el presente." PhD, Universidad del País Vasco, 1996.

Calderón de la Barca, Pedro. *El año santo en Madrid*, edited by Ignacio Arellano and Carlos Mata. Pamplona: Universidad de Navarra, 2005.

Cervantes Saavedra, Miguel de. *Don Quixote*, edited by James H. Montgomery. Indianapolis: Hackett, 2009.

Cox-Rearick, Janet. "Fra Bartolomeo's St. Mark Evangelist and St. Sebastian with an Angel." *Mitteilungen Des Kunsthistorischen Institutes in Florenz* 18, no. 3 (1974): 329-354.

Darwent, Charles. "Arrows of Desire: How did St Sebastian Become an Enduring, Homo-Erotic Icon? - Features, Art - the Independent," accessed 6/21/2011, 2011, http://www.independent.co.uk/arts-entertainment/art/features/arrows-of-desire-how-did-st-sebastian-become-an-enduring-homoerotic-icon-779388.html

DiGangi, Mario. *The Homoerotics of Early Modern Drama*. Cambridge: Cambridge University Press, 1997.

Estenoz y Lodosa, Pedro de. *El soldado más herido y vivo después de muerto*. In *Parte veinte y quatro de comedias nueuas y escogidas de los mejores ingenios de España*, edited by Juan de San Vicente. Madrid: Mateo Fernández de Espinosa Arteag, 1666.

Fantina, Richard. *Ernest Hemingway: Machismo and Masochism*. New York: Palgrave Macmillan, 2005.

Fernandez, Dominique. *A Hidden Love: Art and Homosexuality*. New York: Prestel, 2001.

Fone, Byrne R. S. *Homophobia: A History*. New York: Metropolitan Books, 2000.

Freedberg, David. *The Power of Images: Studies in the History and Theory of Response*. Chicago: University of Chicago Press, 1989.

García Lorca, Federico. *Poet in New York*. Translated by Greg Simon and Steven F. White, edited by Christopher Maurer. New York: Farrar Straus Giroux, 1988.

Giffney, Noreen and Michael O'Rourke. *The Ashgate Research Companion to Queer Theory*. Burlington, VT: Ashgate, 2009.

Goldman, Jason. "Subject of the Visual Arts: St. Sebastian." In *The Queer Encyclopedia of the Visual Arts*, edited by Claude J. Summers, 321-22. San Francisco: Cleis Press, 2004.

Greer, Germaine. *The Beautiful Boy*. New York: Rizzoli International Publications, 2003.

Hagen, Rainer and Rose-Marie Hagen. *What Great Paintings Say*. Köln: Taschen, 2003.

Harris, Max. *Aztecs, Moors, and Christians: Festivals of Reconquest in Mexico and Spain*. Austin: University of Texas Press, 2000.

Hollingsworth, Mary. *Art in World History*. Vol. 2. Armonk, N.Y.: Sharpe Reference, 2004.

Horswell, Michael J. *Decolonizing the Sodomite: Queer Tropes of Sexuality in Colonial Andean Culture*. Austin: University of Texas Press, 2005.

Hutcheson, Gregory S. "The Sodomitic Moor: Queerness in the Narrative of Reconquista." In *Queering the Middle Ages*, edited by Glenn Burger and Steven F. Kruger, 99-122. Minneapolis: University of Minnesota Press, 2001.

Johnson, Carroll B. *Cervantes and the Material World*. Urbana: University of Illinois Press, 2000.

Johnson, Harold. "A Padophile in the Palace or the Sexual Abuse of King Sebastian of Portugal (1554-1578) and its Consequences." In *Pelo Vaso Traseiro: Sodomy and Sodomites in Luso-Brazilian History*, edited by Harold Johnson and Francis A. Dutra, 195-229. Tucson: Fenestra Books, 2006.

Jordan, Mark D. "Saint Pelagius, Ephebe and Martyr." In *Queer Iberia: Sexualities, Cultures, and Crossings from the Middle Ages to the Renaissance*, edited by Josiah Blackmore and Gregory S. Hutcheson, 23-47. Durham: Duke University Press, 1999.

Kaye, Richard. "'Determined Raptures': St. Sebastian and the Victorian Discourse of Decadence." *Victorian Literature and Culture* 27, no. 1 (1999): 269-303.

————. "Losing His Religion: Saint Sebastian as Contemporary Gay Martyr." In *Outlooks: Lesbian and Gay Sexualities and Visual Cultures*, edited by Peter Horne and Reina Lewis, 86-105. New York: Routledge, 1996.

————. "Sebastian, St." In *The Gay and Lesbian Literary Heritage: A Reader's Companion to the Writers and their Works, from Antiquity to the Present*, edited by Claude J. Summers, 606-607. New York: Routledge, 2002.

————. "St. Sebastian: The Uses of Decadence." In *Saint Sebastian: A Splendid Readiness for Death*, edited by Gerald Matt and Wolfgang Fetz, 11-16. Bielefeld: Kerber, 2003.

Leppert, Richard D. *Art and the Committed Eye: The Cultural Functions of Imagery*. Boulder: Westview Press, 1996.

Mann, Richard G. "*GLBTQ: An Encyclopedia of Gay, Lesbian, Bisexual, Transgender, & Queer Culture,* Greco, El (Domenicos Theotocopoulos)," accessed 6/21/2011, 2011, http://www.glbtq.com/arts/greco_e,2.html.

Mariscal, George. "Symbolic Capital in the Spanish Comedia." *Renaissance Drama* 21, (1990): 143-169.

Martín, Adrienne. "Images of Deviance in Cervantes's Algiers." *Cervantes: Bulletin of the Cervantes Society of America* 15, no. 2 (1995): 5-15.

Martorell, Joanot. *Tirant lo Blanc*. Translated by Ray La Fontaine. New York: Peter Lang, 1993.

Matt, Gerald and Wolfgang Fetz. *Saint Sebastian: A Splendid Readiness for Death*. Bielefeld: Kerber, 2003.

Maurer, Christopher. "Prologue." In *Sebastian's Arrows: Letters and Mementos of Salvador Dalí and Federico García Lorca*, 1-27. Chicago: Swan Isle Press, 2004.

Mills, Robert. "Ecce Homo." In *Gender and Holiness: Men, Women, and Saints in Late Medieval Europe*, edited by Samantha Riches and Sarah Salih, 152-173. New York: Routledge, 2002.

————. "'Whatever You Do Is a Delight to Me!': Masculinity, Masochism, and Queer Play in Representations of Male Martyrdom." *Exemplaria: A Journal of Theory in Medieval and Renaissance Studies* 13, no. 1 (2001): 1-37.

Mitchell, Peter. "The Politics of Morbidity: Plague Symbolism in Martyrdom and Medical Anatomy." In *The Arts of 17th-Century Science: Representations of the Natural World in European and North American Culture*, edited by Claire Jowitt and Diane Watt, 77-94. Burlington, VT: Ashgate, 2002.

Monter, E. William. *Frontiers of Heresy: The Spanish Inquisition from the Basque Lands to Sicily*. Cambridge: Cambridge University Press, 1990.

Mornin, Edward and Lorna Mornin. *Saints: A Visual Guide*. Grand Rapids, Mich.: W.B. Eerdmans Pub., 2006.

Morris, David B. *The Culture of Pain*. Berkeley: University of California Press, 1991.

Pacheco, Francisco. *Arte de la pintura*, edited by Francisco J. Sánchez Canón. Madrid: Instituto de Valencia de Don Juan, 1956.

Padrón, Ricardo. "Love American Style: The Virgin Land and the Sodomitic Body in Ercilla's *Araucana*." *Revista de Estudios Hispánicos* 34, no. 3 (2000): 561-584.

Puff, Helmut. "Early Modern Europe, 1400-1700." In *Gay Life and Culture: A World History*, edited by Robert Aldrich, 79-101. New York: Universe, 2006.

Rambuss, Richard. *Closet Devotions*. Durham: Duke University Press, 1998.

Ressouni-Demigneux, Karim. *Saint-Sébastien*. Paris: Regard, 2000.

Rocke, Michael. *Forbidden Friendships: Homosexuality and Male Culture in Renaissance Florence*. Oxford: Oxford University Press, 1996.

Saint-Saëns, Alain. "Homoerotic Suffering, Pleasure, and Desire in Early Modern Europe (1450-1750)." In *Lesbianism and Homosexuality in Early Modern Spain: Literature and Theater in Context*, edited by María José Delgado and Alain Saint-Saëns, 3-86. New Orleans: University Press of the South, 2000.

Saslow, James M. *Pictures and Passions: A History of Homosexuality in the Visual Arts.* New York: Viking, 1999.

———. "The Tenderest Lover: Saint Sebastian in Renaissance Painting. A Proposed Homoerotic Iconology for North Italian Art 1450-1550." *Gai Saber* 1, no. 1 (1977): 58-66.

Savastano, Peter. "St. Gerard Teaches Him that Love Cancels that Out." In *Gay Religion,* edited by Scott Thumma and Edward R. Gray, 181-220. Walnut Creek, CA: AltaMira Press, 2005.

Schroeder, Henry Joseph. *Canons and Decrees of the Council of Trent.* Rockford, Ill.: Tan Books and Publishers, 1978.

Spear, Richard E. *The "Divine" Guido: Religion, Sex, Money, and Art in the World of Guido Reni.* New Haven: Yale University Press, 1997.

Spivey, Nigel Jonathan. *Enduring Creation: Art, Pain, and Fortitude.* Berkeley: University of California Press, 2001.

Stroud, Matthew D. *Plot Twists and Critical Turns: Queer Approaches to Early Modern Spanish Theater.* Lewisburg: Bucknell University Press, 2007.

Talvacchia, Bette. "The Double Life of St. Sebastian in Renaissance Art." In *The Body in Early Modern Italy*, edited by Julia L. Hairston and Walter Stephens, 226-248. Baltimore: Johns Hopkins University Press, 2010.

Vargas Llosa, Mario. *Carta de batalla por Tirant lo Blanc.* Barcelona: Seix Barral, 1991.

Vasari, Giorgio. *Vasari's Lives of Italian Painters*, edited by Havelock Ellis. London: W. Scott, 1895.

Vega, Lope de. *El acero de Madrid*, edited by Aline Bergounioux, Jean Lemartinel and Gilbert Zonana. Paris: Klincksieck, 1971.

Velasco, Sherry M. *Lesbians in Early Modern Spain.* Nashville: Vanderbilt University Press, 2011.

Vélez de Guevara, Luis. *La serrana de la Vera*, edited by Enrique Rodríguez Cepeda. Madrid: Cátedra, 1982.

Walters, Margaret. *The Nude Male: A New Perspective.* New York: Paddington Press, 1978.

Wyke, Maria. "Playing Roman Soldiers: The Martyred Body, Derek Jarman's *Sebastiane*, and the Representation of Male Homosexuality." In *Parchments of Gender: Deciphering the Bodies of Antiquity*, edited by Maria Wyke, 243-266. Oxford: Oxford University Press, 1998.

Zupnick, Irving L. "Saint Sebastian: The Vicissitudes of the Hero as Martyr." In *Concepts of the Hero in the Middle Ages and the Renaissance*, edited by Norman T. Burns and Christopher J. Reagan, 239-267. Albany: State University of New York Press, 1975.

CHAPTER 2

Beyond Don Juan: Different Models of Masculinity in the Peripheral Authors from the Spanish Second Romanticism

Begoña Regueiro-Salgado
Universidad Complutense de Madrid

This chapter explores representations of masculinity in Spain during the second half of the nineteenth century, as presented in a (selected) number of literary works by peripheral Spanish Second Romantics.[1] Looking at these authors and their texts, the paper will identify a number of changes in gender relations at the time, which began in the peripheral parts of Spain, and which may be associated with specific socio-economic conditions differing from those found in central Spain. Although the majority of writers from the Second Romanticism were not from Madrid, many of them met in the capital city of Spain and pursued their literary careers there. There are, however, two major exceptions to this rule, two writers who kept their links with their backgrounds and used their texts to present and defend the characteristics of their homelands. They are Antonio Trueba and Rosalía de Castro, who came from the Basque Country and Galicia, respectively, two communities in which there was a rise in nationalism at the time. Both authors were centrally concerned with showing the rest of Spain the particular characteristics of these regions, including, as we shall see, men and women's patterns of behavior. While my study focuses on these two writers and the new masculine models they portray in their works, it may be necessary to begin by examining certain aspects of the general situation in Spain at that time in order to better understand why these authors created different models of masculinity and gender relations in their texts.

Spain versus "the Peripheries" in the Second Half of the Nineteenth Century

In the first place, one should bear in mind that liberal ideas arrived in Spain in the 1850s, and that together with liberalism came State centralization. Under the new system, Spain was divided into provinces. A representative was sent by the central government in Madrid to every province, with the responsibility of ensuring that the people there abided by the laws of the monarchy. Although liberalism generally went hand in hand with economic growth, this was not the case in every part of Spain. The larger cities like Madrid underwent considerable development, while other regions in Spain did not develop at all, with the result that the gap between Spanish cities grew much wider. Therefore, a lot of citizens questioned the new system and began to see nationalism as an option.

One such region was Galicia. In the 1850s, its population was growing rapidly but it was suffering from underdevelopment. This led to overexploitation of the land, which resulted in even more misery. This combination of difficult circumstances left the Galician people with little choice but to move away or emigrate. This would not be the first time people had emigrated from Galicia. During the first half of the century, for example, many of them had gone to Castile and Andalusia. This time, however, they looked to emigrate further afield and began to move to South America, especially Argentina and Paraguay. As the central government could not come up with any ideas as to how to improve development in Galicia, it began to support emigration. In 1853 it removed all restrictions on emigration, and in 1873 it gave full permission for people to leave, which led to a massive emigration in the 1880s, mostly of men. This had two major consequences for Galicia. On the one hand, there was a growing dissatisfaction with the central government because of its failure to improve the situation in Galicia. On the other, the departure of Galician men made it necessary for certain feminine patterns of behavior to change. In many ways, Galician women had to fulfill the masculine role, even though the place of privilege in the house was kept for the absent man. At any rate, the second half of the nineteenth century in Galician society was characterized by a lack of men, making it necessary for women to play a masculine role. The feminine models of that time in Galicia were characterized by strong women who, as well as doing the housework as "angels in the house," were also required to work on the land and thus do both masculine and feminine work. These solitary women received no support, either at work or in their affective life. In rural societies, gender relations already showed a different construction, but this difference was even more marked in the case of Galicia because of the absence of men.

Moreover, other factors promoting change in gender relations were at play in Galicia. The gender role models professed by the cultured minority, who tried to take part in politics, were different from those of the central Government. For instance, Ramón de la Sagra, a Galician economist who proposed a preindustrial agricultural society for Galicia, advocated utopian socialism and Fourier's ideas in his *Lecciones de economía social*,[2] as Davies and Cambrón-Infante have pointed out. One such idea was that a society's level of progress should be measured by the level of emancipation of its women. Catherine Davies points out that Galician intellectuals also adopted from Spanish Krausism the idea that both partners should work as equals within marriage (291).[3] Thus, both the social situation and the ideologies supported by intellectuals helped to create an alternative recognition of gender roles, which would be reflected, as will be shown, in the works of Rosalía de Castro.[4]

As regards the Basque Country, the situation there was not all that different. Enriqueta Sesmero-Cutanda—who has studied the input of Basque women to their community by examining material, immaterial, and symbolic contributions to the patrimony—has shown how the role of women developed far beyond domestic tasks, thus illustrating, once again, a difference in sexual roles with respect to the rest of the country.[5] Although not to the same extent as Galicia, the Basque Country also experienced temporary emigration; each year, many men left the Basque Country for a few months to look for work in other parts of Spain. During the same period of this particularly belligerent century, several civil wars and a number of military uprisings took place in Spain. Three civil wars–the Carlist Wars–were fought in the nineteenth century, in particular in the Basque Country. These wars were ostensibly about the succession of the monarchy, but there was something of more significance underlying them. The confrontation was not between two possible monarchs, but between traditional values (defended by Carlos, Fernando VII's brother) and liberal ideas (defended by the legitimate Queen, Isabel II). This affected all the provinces of Spain that had their own regional laws or "*fueros*." During the last years of his reign, Fernando VII had allowed some reforms, including the equalizing of laws and customs all over Spain, and had eliminated the "*fueros*."[6] Prince Carlos, on the other hand, promised to give back the "fueros." This provided him with the support of provinces like the Basque Country and Navarra. The significance of this for us is that these wars meant that large numbers of Basque men, whether voluntarily or not,[7] enlisted in the Carlist army, leaving their land and property under the protection of their wives, who developed a capacity for solving problems and adjusting to change. Once more, some of the roles they adopted were, predictably, masculine.

At the same time, the particular laws of the Basque Country had already put men and women on a more equal footing. To begin with, as Oihane Oliveri-Korta points out, the transmission of inheritance from parents to children was not the same there as in the rest of Spain. The person who would inherit the family house and its contents could be freely designated in the Basque Country, which meant it could be inherited by either a woman or a man. Whoever it was, the new owner's spouse had to move to the house and make a financial contribution. Basque women were thus treated equally and had their own belongings, while elsewhere in Spain women depended on men, initially on their fathers and then on their husbands or brothers.[8]

There was yet another crucial factor affecting gender relations in the Basque Country. Although the Basque Country had by that time already been reached by industrialization, especially in the cities, the society continued to be largely preindustrial. In that society domestic duties associated with women and external duties associated with men would thus become mixed, given the diversity of activities and economic responsibilities that had to be assumed.[9] In the Basque Country, women also took part in major economic transactions, even though no help was provided by the central State because, as Davis points out, kings used to believe that women's obedience to their husbands encouraged submission to the centralization of the State.[10] According to Davis, they saw obedient women as a model of submission within the family that would, in turn, foster submission of all the family to the central State.[11]

From all this, one may conclude, then, that the situation of gender relations in Galicia and the Basque Country was at least slightly different from the dominant "angel in the house" model of Spain at the time. Also, the characteristics shown by such "marginal" women went beyond the classical "feminine" virtues of sensitivity, tenderness, and modesty, celebrated by intellectuals or politicians such as Severo Catalina,[12] and supported by the medical theories of doctors like Pedro Felipe Monlau (1865), who defined woman as a human being created and adapted solely for the purposes of motherhood.[13]

It would seem, then, that nineteenth-century gender patterns were not homogeneous throughout Spain. However, do the authors who attacked the model of the "angel in the house" say anything about masculine models? They do, indeed. If we analyze the works of Rosalía de Castro and Antonio

Trueba, we will find men whose masculinity differs radically from the hegemonic model. This seems to have much to do, as we shall see, with the social differences found in Galicia and the Basque Country that have been mentioned above.

Alternative Models of Masculinity in the Works of Rosalía de Castro and Antonio Trueba

For analytic purposes, the different male characters portrayed by Rosalía de Castro and Antonio Trueba will be classified here into the following groups: a) absent men; b) men who take on feminine roles; and c) men who challenge the Don Juan archetype.[14]

Absent Men

While these types of men are not very innovative, they are important inasmuch as their absence brings changes to society and causes gender roles to change —even when women keep them in mind and keep their places free for their return. It is quite usual in de Castro's works to find references to men who have to emigrate for economic reasons. Sometimes, these men are described simply from a neutral point of view that sympathizes with them —and not only with them, but also with their lonely wives. At other times, however, they appear not as victims but as culprits. In these cases, the author emphasizes the lack of loyalty in these men, who are abroad with other women and have no intention of going back, while their wives are suffering all alone in Galicia. One example of this is the poem "*¿Qué lle digo?*" ("What Shall I Tell Her?"), from the fifth part of *Follas Novas*. In this poem, we find both models of men. On the one hand, we see a man who is about to go back to Galicia, having worked hard as an emigrant; on the other, there is his friend, who does not intend to go back because he is richer abroad and has met another woman. The man who is about to return asks his friend what he should say to his wife, who is waiting for him at home. After making it clear that he prefers to be free (without children, with more money, and with new women), the message his friend wants sent to his wife is simply that she will have to take care of herself:

> —Déixate de concencias e delores,
> que non teñen lugare
> tratando de mulleres e de amores.

Que ela vexa, se quer, de se curare;
e cóntalle que cando eu o tivere,
xa lle darei con que se procurare.
I agora, ¡adios!, ¡hastra que Dios quixere![15]

Men Who Take On Feminine Roles

In order to fully understand what we mean by "feminine" men, we will first have to review the traits that were traditionally linked to women at the time, since the same traits appear linked to "feminized" male characters. Here are two (archetypical) testimonies from the nineteenth century that attempted to define women. Fermín Gonzalo Morán, for example, wrote the following in an article entitled "La mujer" (*El Correo de la Moda*, November 10, 1877):

> Nególe el cielo a la mujer la fuerza y la energía física e intelectual que concediera al hombre, pero dotóla en cambio ricamente de una imaginación vivaz y creadora, de un corazón sensible y generoso.[16]

Similarly, Clarín, the reputed Spanish realist writer, defended the close links between femininity, on the one hand, and fantasy and sensitivity, on the other, suggesting that "Una mujer que sueña es una mujer que piensa de la manera más natural de pensar las mujeres."[17] Dissociating women from reason and rationality, he thus insisted that:

> El instrumento que mueve a la mujer la mayoría de las veces es la ilusión, la fantasía y el ensueño. La mujer de sensibilidad, la eternamente femenina, transforma la realidad mediante la emoción y la evocación de sus vivencias.[18]

It would seem, then, that the characteristics that made women different from men were sensitivity, imagination, dreams, illusion, fantasy, reverie, etc. In view of this, one could already conclude that all poets, according to the definitions of the Second Romantics, were actually provided with a "feminine" soul, since they were traditionally defined by their special capacity for feeling. Indeed, poets, as Rosalía de Castro wrote, feel differently from the rest:

> Los poetas son seres distintos de los demás, no sienten como todos sienten y por eso no los comprenden todos. He aquí por qué siempre oculté a miradas extrañas lo que pasaba en el fondo de mi corazón.[19]

Likewise, Selgas-Carrasco states that poets feel everybody's sadness, suggesting, for example, that "este desgraciado tiene el alma en todas partes porque su oficio es sentir las penas de los demás."[20] Another similar example is provided by Bécquer, who also described Manrique, one of the poets in his work, as one who loved being alone because this way he could give free rein to his imagination:

> Amaba la soledad porque en su seno, dando rienda suelta a la imaginación, forjaba un mundo fantástico, habitado por extrañas creaciones, hijas de sus delirios y sus ensueños de poeta, porque Manrique era poeta.[21]

As well as these examples, an extremely interesting character for studying the "feminine soul" in men is Flavio, from Rosalía de Castro's work of the same name (*Flavio*, 1861), whose role in the novel, according to March (*De musa*, 142-143) might as well have been played by a kid or a woman. Indeed, Flavio, as March (151) suggests, shows most of the defining features of a nineteenth-century heroine: spirituality, full commitment to love, patient suffering, and extreme sensitivity, even to the extent of putting his life in danger. Indeed, he is an excellent example in all these respects. Therefore, when the narrator says that he has a "poet's imagination,"[22] and that he is "voluble y ligero en cierto modo, como todos los poetas, e impresionable hasta la exageración,"[23] he is clearly describing features that were normally assigned to women. We also see him as being almost "hysterical," another feature that was usually associated with the heroines of nineteenth-century novels:

> Flavio agitaba el látigo con su brazo infatigable. Su mirada, extraviada, no alcanzaba a distinguir entre los densos vapores si caminaba por la ancha y fácil carretera, o si su carruaje rodaba a orillas de un precipicio, y su convulsa mano no podía detener ya lo desbocados caballos.[24]

Another very interesting feature of Flavio is how he evolves with respect to his participation in society. At the beginning of the novel, Flavio lives in a palace completely alone, since both of his parents have recently died. This is the time when he decides to leave the house in order to feel free and see the world. In his first contact with the village people, he is described as a "voluntad virgen" ("a virgin will") and it is at this point especially that he behaves like a woman, especially when he meets Mara and falls in love with her. Later, however, he enters society and his behavior gradually changes. First, he takes on a bourgeois role, trying to make Mara change and become another "angel in the house:"[25]

> ¡Si supieras cuánta ternura, cuán dulce sentimiento inspira el rostro de una mujer bañado por las lágrimas...! ¡Cuánto es amada la que se resigna a sufrir cuando es

olvidada...! ¡Cuando se la ve descender hasta la misma tumba amando los recuerdos que la hacen morir...! ¡He aquí la poesía de la mujer! Si os avergonzáis, pues, de amar, Mara, renegad de una vez para siempre de vuestro sexo...; si por el contrario, queréis cumplir vuestro destino, olvidad el mundo y amad a Flavio.[26]

The more Flavio participates in society, the more he seems to adopt hegemonic masculinity. However, this hegemonic masculinity needs to be reinforced by his relationship with the other sex. In order to strengthen his masculinity, he needs Mara to act according to the rules of traditional femininity, since when she acts the way she is, he feels insecure. Thus, he asks her to act as an "angel in the house" who simply loves, suffers in love, and cries, lacking autonomy or subjectivity. At the end of the novel, Flavio goes even further and becomes a kind of Don Juan, who abandons Mara, gets a young girl pregnant (she finally kills herself because of him), and starts a relationship with an old woman just for her money:

Ella es vieja y horrible, pero tiene ocho millones de capital y él no ha vacilado en vender por ella su libertad. Una pobre niña víctima suya, que le esperaba creyendo casarse con él, se ha suicidado con su pequeño hijo al saber la infausta nueva.[27]

Flavio's evolution thus reveals two important aspects. In the first place, it shows he is not permanently committed to a particular pattern of masculinity but changes from one type of masculine behavior (the bourgeois role) to another (the "Don Juan"), depending on the situation. Thus, his change also illustrates the social construction of gender roles, both masculine and feminine, for, as has been suggested, Flavio's gradual change depends on his increasing involvement with society and its rules. He begins to act violently to cover a sensitivity that would make him look weak to the society (March, *De musa*, 151).

Besides Flavio, Rosalía created other masculine characters as well, who, like Flavio (at least before entering society), are depicted as equally feminine. One example is Luis, from *El Primer Loco* (1881), who stands out from the rest of men for his imagination, and who is thus compared to the Romantic poet Hoffmann:

Fluctuando siempre entre lo real y lo fantástico, entre lo absurdo y lo sublime, dijérase que hablaba como escribía Hoffmann.[28]

Because of this imagination, he is even seen by other people as mad:

Ignoro si en realidad es o no un loco sublime; pero fuerza es convenir, por lo menos, en que posee una imaginación poderosa.[29]

Clearly, then, Luis embodies the model of the Romantic poet. Later, when he falls in love with Berenice, he also adopts a feminine model of behavior, while she teases him and laughs at his unusual romantic attitude. Other similar characters are the Duke of Glory in *El Caballero de las Botas Azules* (1867), a strangely undefined character who attempts to change society, especially the role of bourgeois women in it, and the muse, who appears in the Prologue to the same book, entitled "Un hombre y una musa" ("A Man and a Muse"). Interestingly, the muse is almost a hybrid creature, who lacks a clear sexual definition —"considera que soy musa, pero no dama"[30]— , and who is described in the following terms:

> Su rostro es largo, ovalado y de una expresión ambigua: tiene los ojos pardos, verdes y azules y parecen igualmente dispuestos a hacer guiños picarescamente o a languidecer de amor. Un fino bozo sombrea el labio superior de su boca algo abultado, pero semejante a una granada entreabierta, mientras dos largas trenzas de cabellos le caen sobre la mórbida espalda medio desnuda.[31]

When the man finally sees the muse, he cannot help being amazed at the view, "¿Conque mi musa era un mari-macho, un ser anfibio de esos que debieran quedar en el vacío para siempre?"[32] The great significance of the Duke and the muse is that they both come to change nineteenth-century society and literature by questioning the traditional patterns of masculinity or femininity. According to Catherine Davies,[33] *El caballero*, the Duke, embodies a number of Krausist attitudes and values: secularism, moral integrity, tolerance, charity, social responsibility and education, as they were defined and defended in Julián Sanz del Río's notes about Krause's work *Ideal de la Humanidad para la vida* (1860).[34] What is interesting for us is the way Rosalía linked Krausism and new gender patterns, selecting his *Caballero*, the Duke, to embody a feminist ideology that wants to change both men and women. Interestingly, then, Rosalía de Castro used indefinite sexual roles and sexually ambiguous characters to defend her new ideas about literature and society. In this way, new roles earmarked for gender, or simply the absence of earmarked roles, were strongly linked to a new society.

Beyond Don Juan: Deconstructing the Archetype

New times demand new heroes. Just as people change according to their times and social conditions, so does the construction of masculinity. Accordingly, when Spanish society changed, its heroes also had to change, especially in those peripheral places where change, as has been suggested, was taking place more quickly. The first Romantics felt the need to defend their individuality and freedom, which they considered to be greater than their role or place in society. They claimed their individuality by asserting their inner life, their freedom, and their independence from society. In the second half of the nineteenth century, when the second Romantics were writing, conditions in Spain had changed. People had become weary of revolution and war and were looking for peace and quiet by the reconstruction of a national cultural identity. In order to achieve it, they resorted to German philosophy and Historical Romanticism, as well as the concept of the *Volksgeist*, which appeared in the works of some German intellectuals in the lasts years of eighteenth century and the early nineteenth century. This idea emrged from the work of Herder, Wolf and, especially, from the conferences that A. W Schlegel read in Vienna between 1808 and 1812. Nicolás Böhl de Faber and later Agustín Durán brought it to Spain, where it is accepted by the Conservative Romanticism, related then to the Romantic German Historical School. According to *Volksgeist* ideology, the "soul," *el alma*, can be found in national cohesive forces that are predicated upon a return to established scales of values and an unconditional adherence to Catholic tradition. It placed a strong emphasis upon the soil, the humble people, their customs, dress, personal and household decoration, architecture and cultural products and, above all, religion and language.[35] There was therefore no longer a need for an individual player like Don Juan, a player that had been imitated so much as to become ridiculous. What were now needed were characters who helped regenerate society.

Because of this change of model, virtually all the authors from the Second Spanish Romanticism created parody characters that helped destroy the Don Juan archetype. In this sense, it becomes particularly interesting to see the ways in which the writer Antonio Trueba moved away from the traditional gender models by condemning male behaviors that might end up hurting women, or even society as a whole. Indeed, in his books we find a total rejection of traditionally "masculine" behaviors, such as infidelity, alcoholism, gender violence, and gambling. Acknowledging the importance of men's respect for women, he defended the equality between men and women within the home and the family, which was very much in line, as has been seen, with the particularly progressive model of gender relations in the Basque Country in the nineteenth century. Examples of this are found in many of his books, but I have chosen two examples in which he emphasizes gender equality in the Basque Country. In *Mari-Santa* (1874), for instance, he defends women's power over the household. Indeed, he supports those husbands who let their wives wield this power, against those who attack them for it. As he wrote:

> Suelen las gentes de criterio superficial acusar a los aldeanos de Vizcaya de que dan excesivo, y por tanto perjudicial, predominio a su mujer sobre ellos, la casa y la familia. Yo tengo por injusta esta afirmación: es verdad que allí la mujer ejerce este predominio; pero no lo es que este predominio sea perjudicial, y por tanto excesivo. Es, por el contrario, muy beneficioso y justo, y para demostrarlo sólo aduciré una razón, aunque pudiera aducir muchas; donde, como sucede en las comarcas cantábricas, la mujer comparte con el marido, en proporción a lo que buenamente permite su sexo y sus fuerzas, el trabajo material, ¿qué sería la mujer si el marido no le recompensase esta ayuda consintiéndole el predominio moral sobre él, la casa y la familia? Sería una miserable esclava, cuya condición reprueban el sentido común, la naturaleza y la religión, que con tan entrañable fe se profesa en aquellas honradas comarcas.[36]

In the tale "El Desarreglo del Mundo" ("The Disarray of the World"), Jesus Christ is asked to fix a number of things when he comes back to the World. One of them is the situation in a little village, in which the women love their husbands so much that the latter take advantage of their love. Indeed, the men continually cheat on the women, since they know their wives will never abandon them. Faced with this, Jesus addresses the men as follows:

> Compañera y no esclava...le dieron a usted ante el altar, y una sola carne y un solo hueso son usted y ella. Ámela usted, séale fiel, que, si así no lo hiciere, su lecho será de espinas, y bajará al sepulcro sin posteridad que le llore y bendiga.[37]

Conclusion

As has been seen, certain masculine models in works from the Second Spanish Romanticism seem to break away from the traditional repertoire of masculine behaviors at the time. Because both Antonio Trueba and Rosalía de Castro lived in the nineteenth century, it may be inappropriate to define them as "feminists," which is a much more contemporary term. However, it is equally important to recognize that that the twentieth-century mentality has specific historical antecedents. The roots of feminism may be traced back to the nineteenth century, when authors like Rosalía de Castro and Antonio Trueba began to portray the first steps towards change. As Susan Kirkpatrick reminds us, "Rosalía de Castro...was not an activist in terms of public or even private demonstrations of feminist convictions. Her writing, however, powerfully registers her lack of conformity with a gender system she perceived as unjust."[38]

Of course, neither Rosalía de Castro nor Antonio Trueba were feminists, but they grew up in "margin-al" backgrounds, Galicia and the Basque Country, where traditional communities had not yet disappeared and where there was a growing concern, as we have seen, over the gender roles assigned by the dominant society. Clearly, the bourgeois mentality constructed the idea of "angel in the house" as if only one social class existed, that of the bourgeoisie, thus failing to take into account the situation of other women, particularly working-class and country women.[39] But both Rosalía de Castro and Antonio Trueba grew up in regions where the social, economic, and even ideological conditions were different. Coming from rural societies where women worked together with men, both writers lived in societies where the lack of men caused women to take "masculine" roles. Thus, they knew that women could be strong and smart and not just sweet and tender, and that gender models could move beyond those imposed by the bourgeoisie. And they reflected it in their fictions. Thus, while neither Rosalía de Castro nor Antonio Trueba marked the end of the feminist revolution, it should also be acknowledged that, without them, some steps towards gender equality may have never been taken.

Notes

[1] By Second Spanish Romanticism, I mean the literary tendency that appeared in Spain around 1850 as a result of the reaction against the First Romanticism. The writers who belonged to this group were born between 1821 (Antonio Trueba) and 1837 (Rosalía de Castro). They grew up with the success of the First Romanticism and began to write when an artistic and literary change was felt to be increasingly necessary. Included in this group are Antonio Trueba (1821-1889), José Selgas y Carrasco (1822-1882), Manuel Cañete (1822-1891), Eulogio Florentino Sanz (1825? -1881), Ángel María Dacarrete (1827-1904), Antonio Arnao (1828-1889), Vicente Barrantes (1829-1898), Juan Antonio de Viedma (1831-1869), Luis García Luna (1834?- 1867?), Arístides Pongilioni (1835-1882), Narciso Campillo (1835-1900), Augusto Ferrán (1835? -1880), Gustavo Adolfo Bécquer (1836-1870), Julio Nombela (1836-1919) and Rosalía de Castro (1837-1885).

[2] *Lecciones de economía social* was read in the Ateneo in 1839. See De La Sagra, "Lecciones."

[3] Davies, "A ideoloxía," 291. According to Davies ("A ideoloxía," 143), in Rosalía's time Krausism meant defending Utopic Socialism, religious freedom, free market, and universal suffrage. Thus, getting involved in this ideology also meant getting involved with democracy and social reformism. For further information about Krausism and Fourierism in Spain, see Gil-Cremades, *Krausistas*; Cambrón-Infante, *El socialismo*; De la Sagra, ibid.

[4] Catherine Davies (*Rosalía*) has explored nineteenth-century Galician history focusing on social, political, and economic issues. Also, Díaz (*La protesta*) explains the economic situation of Galicia at that time. On the economic situation in nineteenth-century Spain in general, see Tuñón de Lara, *La España*.

5   Sesmero-Cutanda, "La mujer," 331-366.

6   The "*fueros*" were legal statutes applicable to a particular locality, which established a set of rules, rights, and privileges generally intended to regulate the local community.

7   Antonio Trueba (who defined himself as against the Carlists) mentions in some of his works that many men were forced to join the Carlist army. For example, in *Cuentos del hogar* (1875), he writes: "Los batallones carlistas de las Provincias Vascongadas se componen casi en su totalidad de forzosos, a pesar de que el pretendiente tiene la poca vergüenza de llamarles voluntarios" (Trueba, *Obras VIII*, 141). "The carlist army from the Basque Country is composed almost totally with forced soldiers, even though the *pretendiente* dares to call them volunteers." He also explains that he had to leave his homeland when he was a young boy and stay away for several years to avoid being recruited by them: "sabes cuál ha sido mi vida…desde que, casi niño, abandoné por primera vez los valles nativos, para que el bando carlista no me obligara a tomar las armas a su favor, cosa que nos repugnaba profundamente a mis padres y a mí (*Obras VIII*, 4-5). "You know how my life has been…, from the time when, being almost a kid I had to abandon my homeland to avoid the carlist making me join them, what my parents and me deeply disliked."

8   Oliveri-Korta, "De hijas," 375.

9   Sesmero-Cutanda, ibid.," 343-344 and 347-348.

10 Davis, "El mundo," 63.

11 Many Basque Country women were performing laboring activities as well. It is not easy to find evidence for this because the people designated by the State to register laboring activities used to link women to the activities of their related men (fathers, brothers, husbands, etc.). However, looking at the 1860 census in Bermeo, for example, one can see that some women provided their own profession, even though it was subsequently deleted (Sesmero-Cutanda, "La mujer," 342).

12 Severo Catalina says: "El secreto de la educación no consiste en formar mujeres sabias: debe consistir en formar mujeres modestas". "The main secret of educations is not creating intelligent woman: it must be create modest woman" (*La mujer*, 115).

13 Pedro Felipe Monlau states: "La matriz es el órgano más importante en la vida de una mujer; es uno de los polos de la organización femenina...En la matriz retumban indefectiblemente todas las afecciones físicas y morales de la mujer, el útero hace que la mujer sea lo que es" (*Higiene*, 129). "Matrix is the most important organ in women's life; it is one of the main points for female organization…Every moral or physical affection of the woman rumbles in her matrix, uterus makes the woman the way she is."

14 Before classifying the new masculinity models we find in the works of these two authors from the Second Romanticism, it should be pointed out that in both cases their characters seem to illustrate, interestingly enough, Connell's (postmodern) view of masculinity whereby "men are not permanently committed to a particular pattern of masculinity. Rather, they make situationally specific choices from a cultural repertoire of masculine behavior" (*Masculinities*, xix, xx). As we shall see, neither Rosalía's nor Trueba's characters follow the same pattern of masculinity all the time but change depending on the situation, or the extent to which they are integrated in society (as in the case of Flavio in the eponymous novel by Rosalía de Castro).

15 Castro, *Obras II*, 428: "Forget conscience and pain/ which do not matter/ when they concern women and love./If she wants, she'll try to cure herself;/and tell her that whenever I've got something/ I will give her something to live on./ And now, Goodbye! See you whenever God wills it!"

16 Aldaraca, *El Ángel*, 69: "Heaven denied to Woman the strength and physical and intellectual energy it gave to Man, but, in exchange, it gave her a creative and lively imagination and a sensitive and generous heart."

17   Clarín, *Obras*, 1069: "A woman who dreams is a woman who thinks in the most natural way in which women think."

18   Clarín, ibid., 1069: "The instrument that moves women most of the times is illusion, fantasy, reverie. The sensitive woman, the one who is always feminine, changes reality through emotion and the evocation of her experiences."

19   Castro, *Obras*, 389: "Poets are different human beings; they do not feel the same as everybody else and that is why not everybody understands them. That is why I always kept what was happening inside my heart well hidden from strange looks."

20   Selgas, *Hojas*, 224: "The soul of this poor man is everywhere because his job is to feel everybody else's sadness."

21   Bécquer, *Obras*, 155: "He loved being alone because then, by giving free rein to his imagination, he created a fantastic world where strange creatures, children of his poet's delirium and fantasies, lived, for Manrique was a poet."

22   Castro, *Obras*, 238.

23   Castro, ibid., 289: "somewhat fickle and flippant, like all poets, and impressionable to the point of exaggeration."

24   Castro, ibid., 265: "Flavio waved the whip with his tireless arm. His eyes, with their faraway look, could not make out through the thick vapor whether he was traveling along the wide easy road or whether his carriage was rolling on the edge of a precipice, and his convulsed hand could no longer stop the runaway horses."

25   Mara is one of Rosalía's most interesting female characters. She has been studied and related to feminism by March because of her defense of women's freedom to choose how they want to be instead of making themselves into what men desire. According to March, Mara´s mistake is being afraid of the society (*De musa*, 146) and accepting some behaviors of Flavio, but she defends feminist ideas as radical as the ones defended by women writers from other countries (March, *De musa*, 150, 152). In the novel, Mara is more rational than Flavio and she rejects being an object of desire for the male characters (Flavio and Ricardo), which is understood as an "unfeminine" attitude. Finally, she has an explicit feminist reaction when she decides not to break away from her social life to go to live with Flavio (March, *De musa*, 152).

26   Castro, *Obras I*, 431: "If you only knew how much tenderness and what sweet feelings are inspired by a woman's face bathed in tears…! How much she is loved, the woman who is resigned to suffering when she is forgotten! When you see her, going to her grave even, still cherishing the memories that are killing her! Here indeed is the poetry of women! If you are ashamed of loving, Mara, deny your sex forever…if, on the other hand, you want to fulfill your destiny, then forget the world and love Flavio."

27   Ibid., 463: "She is old and ugly, but she has a capital of eight million and he has not hesitated to sell his freedom for her. A poor girl, a victim of his, who was waiting for him believing she was going to marry him, killed herself and her little child on learning the terrible news."

28   Ibid., 677: "Always wavering between reality and fantasy, between the absurd and the sublime, you could say that he spoke as Hoffman wrote."

29   Ibid., 677: "I do not know if he actually is a sublime fool or not, but at least we have to agree he has a powerful imagination."

30   Ibid., 3: "Consider me a muse, but not a lady."

31   Ibid., 17: "His face is long and oval-shaped and he has an ambiguous expression: he has brown, green and blue eyes that look just as ready to wink mischievously as to languish with love. A fine moustache makes a shadow over his thickish upper lip, which looks like a half open pomegranate, while two long braids fall over his soft half naked back."

32   Ibid., 17: "So my muse was a virago, one of those amphibious beings who should stay in a void forever?"

33   Davies, ibid., 281-284.

34   Julián Sanz del Río spread Krausist ideas in Spain through his lessons at the University and through his edition of Krause's texts in 1860.

35   Cardwell, *History*, 159-177.

36   Trueba, *Mari-Santa*, 174: "Superficial people accuse villagers from Vizcaya of giving excessive, and therefore harmful, power to their wives over themselves, their homes and their families. I think this opinion is unfair: it is true that women there have this power, but it is not true that it is harmful, and therefore excessive. It is, on the contrary, very beneficial and fair, and to prove it I will give just one reason, even though I could give many: in the region of Cantabria, where the woman shares the physical work with her husband, insofar as her sex and her strength allow, what would become of the woman if her husband did not reward her by giving her moral predominance over him, their household and their family? She would be a miserable slave, in a condition condemned by common sense, nature and the religion they profess with such a deep faith in those honest villages."

37   Trueba, *Obras X*, 195: "They gave you a partner at the altar, not a slave, and she and you are the same flesh and the same bone. Love her, be faithful to her, because if you do not, you will have a bed of thorns and will go to the tomb with nobody to cry for you and bless you."

38   Kirkpatrick, *Las Románticas*, 296.

39   Aldaraca, ibid., 64.

Bibliography

Aldaraca, Bridget. *El Ángel del hogar. Galdós and the Ideology of Domesticity in Spain*, Valencia: Artes Gráficas Soler, 1991.

Bécquer, Gustavo Adolfo. *Obras Completas*, edited by Joan Estruch Tobella. Madrid: Cátedra, 2004.

Cambrón-Infante, Ascensión, *El socialismo racional de Ramón de la Sagra*, A Coruña: Deputación Provincial, 1989.

Cardwell, Richard A. *History and Historiography: Joan Maragall and the Search for Roots*. Roma: Studi Ispanici, Intituti editoriali e poligrafini internazionali, 2005.

Castells, Luis and Antonio Rivera. "Vida cotidiana y nuevos comportamientos sociales (El País Vasco, 1876-1923). *Revista Ayer de la Asociación de Historia Contemporánea* 19 (1995): http://www.ahistcon.org/docs/ayer/ayer19_06.pdf

Castro, Rosalía de. *Obras completas, I y II*. Madrid: Biblioteca Castro, 1993.

Catalina, Severo. *La mujer, apuntes para un libro*. Madrid: San Martín, 1861.

Clarín, Leopolodo "Alas." *Obras Selectas*, edited by Juan Antonio Cabezas. Madrid: Biblioteca Nueva, 1947.

Connell, R.W. *Masculinities*. Berkley and Los Angeles: University of California Press, 2005.

Davies, Catherine "A ideoloxía político-social de Rosalía: Raíz do seu pesimismo existencial." *Actas do congreso internacional de estudios sobre Rosalía de Castro e o seu tempo*, edited by Servicio de Publicacións da Universidade de Santiago de Compostela, 299-306. Santiago de Compostela: Consello da Cultura Galega e Universidade de Santiago de Compostela, 1986.

———. *Rosalía de Castro e o seu tempo*. Galáxia: Vigo, 1987.

Davis, Natalie Z. "El mundo al revés: las mujeres en el poder." *Historia y género. Las mujeres en la Europa moderna y contemporánea*, edited by James Amelang and Mary Nash, 59-92. Valencia: Edicions Alfons el Magnànim, 1990.

De la Sagra, Ramón. "Lecciones de economía social." *Reis: Revista Española de Investigaciones Sociológicas*, No. 88 (Oct.-Dec., 1999), pp. 273-294, Centro de Investigaciones Sociológicas: www.jstor.org/stable/40184211

Gil-Cremades, Juan José. *Krausistas y liberales*. Madrid: Seminarios y Ediciones, 1975.

Imízcoz-Beunza, José María, ed. *Casa, familia y sociedad (País Vasco, España, América, s. XV-XIX)*. Bilbao: Servicio de Publicaciones de la Universidad del País Vasco, 2004.

Kirkpatrick, Susan. *Las Románticas, Women Writers and Subjectivity in Spain, 1835-1850*. Berkeley: University of California Press, 1989.

Krause, Karl. *Ideal de la humanidad para la vida*. Introduction and notes by Julián Sanz del Río. Madrid: Imp. De F. Martínez García, 1871.

March, Kathleen. N. *De musa a literata: el feminismo en la narrativa de Rosalía de Castro*. Sada, A Coruña: Ediciós do Castro, 1994.

Monlau, Pedro Felipe. *Higiene del matrimonio o el libro de los casados*, 3ª ed. Madrid: M. Rivadeneyra, 1865.

Oliveri-Korta, Oihane. "De hijas, herederas y señoras. Mujer y *oeconómica*: Algunas reflexiones para una investigación." In *Casa, familia y sociedad (País Vasco, España, América, s. XV-XIX)*, edited by José María Imízcoz-Beunza, 367-394. Bilbao: Servicio de Publicaciones de la Universidad del País Vasco, 2004.

Regueiro-Salgado, Begoña. *La poética del Segundo Romanticismo español*. Madrid: FUE, 2010.

Selgas-Carrasco, José. *Hojas sueltas Texto impreso: viajes ligeros alrededor de varios asuntos*. Madrid: Centro General de Administración, 1861.

Sesmero-Cutanda, E. "La mujer y la casa: reflexiones metodológicas sobre el aporte económico femenino al hogar rural popular de Vizcaya (fines del siglo XVI-ca. 1876)." In *Casa, familia y sociedad (País Vasco, España, América, s. XV-XIX)*, edited by J.M. Imízcoz-Beunza, 331-366. Bilbao: Servicio de Publicaciones de la Universidad del País Vasco, 2004.

Trueba, Antonio. *Mari-Santa, cuadros de un hogar y sus contornos*. Madrid: A. de Carlos e hijo editores, 1874.

———. *Obras VIII: Cuentos del hogar*. Madrid: Antonino Romero, 1905.

———. *Obras X: Cuentos populares de Vizcaya*. Madrid: Antonino Romero, 1905.

Tuñón de Lara, Manuel. *La España del siglo XIX*. Barcelona: Laia, 1975.

CHAPTER 3
A Galician Werewolf in Spain: Contemporary Representations of Manuel Blanco Romasanta

Danny M. Barreto
Vassar College

Stories of people transformed into wolves have been used in Western societies since antiquity to express a range of cultural anxieties about voracious sexuality, the predatory nature of humanity or mankind's connection to the animal. The werewolf has long held a place of particular cultural importance within Galicia, "a rexión de España na que as lendas e as historias orais sobre licántropos tiveron, quizá, maior difusión popular e un tratamento literario culto que lle outorgou unha difusión máis ampla."[1] The Galician folk imagination is filled with stories in which people are transformed permanently or temporarily into wolves: seventh or ninth-born males without any sisters in between,[2] as well as the men and women who are victims of a "fada" (curses) or "bruxería" (witchcraft), as has been detailed by in a number of anthropological and ethnographic works.[3] Over the twentieth century, the werewolf has moved beyond just oral folktales. Many of the region's most important writers, such as Vicente Risco, Emilia Pardo Bazán, Ánxel Fole, and Celso Emilio Ferreiro have written about werewolves. Risco, in his 1929 speech to the Real Academia Galega entitled "Un caso de lycantropía. O home-lobo," claimed that "o mito do lobishome é unha peza honorable no noso limpo brasón,"[4] taking the figure of the werewolf as a central theme and symbol of a traditional, ethnic, and atavistic part of Galician identity as he would do in some of his fiction as well.[5] Entire conferences, such as *O mito que fascina: do lobo ao lobishome* (*The Fascinating Myth: from the Wolf to the Wolf-man*) organized by the Asociación de Escritores en Lingua Galega (AELG) in 2009, and recent volumes such as archaeologist David Pérez-López's *Os foxos do lobo. A caza do lobo na cultura popular* (*The Wolf Traps. The Hunt for the Wolf in Popular Culture*) (2010), have emphasized the importance of the wolf within all aspects of Galician social life. Just how emblematic the werewolf has become of official Galician cultural discourse can be seen in *O Camiño das estrelas* (*The Path of the Stars*) (1993) by director Chano Piñeiro, a 34-minute film sponsored by the Xunta to promote tourism. The film tells the love story of a werewolf and a mermaid—another mythical, half-human/half-animal hybrid closely associated with Galician nationalism[6]—who serve as tour guides throughout the Galician countryside and offer forth a traditionalist vision of Galician culture.[7]

There is one particular werewolf whose tale has been retold by writers, critics, and directors for more than a century and a half.[8] Manuel Blanco Romasanta, the self-proclaimed lycanthrope who claimed the lives of as many as thirteen victims between 1843 and 1852, has become the stuff of modern legends. He haunts the region's folktales and ghost stories where he appears under any number of sobriquets: *el sacamantecas, o sacauntos, el hombre del saco, el hombre lobo, o lobishome,* etc. Additionally, as anthropologist Xosé Ramón Mariño-Ferro points out, Romasanta has become a case study for doctors, psychiatrists, lawyers, and philosophers, both past and present.[9] Writers and filmmakers continue to revisit the tale, offering different versions and interpretations of the real life wolf-man. I am presently concerned with four works—two novels and their film adaptations—that appear over the course of the twentieth century. The first pair comprises the novel *El bosque de Ancines* (*The Forest of Ancines*) (1947) by Carlos Martínez-Barbeito and the film *El bosque del lobo* (*The Forest of the Wolf*) (1970), directed by Pedro Olea and starring José Luis López-Vázquez. The second, Alfredo Conde's Galician-language novel, *Romasanta. Memorias incertas do home lobo* (*Romasanta. The Uncertain Memoirs of the Wolf-Man*) (2004) and director Paco Plaza's English-language film adaptation, *Romasanta: The Werewolf Hunt* (2004).

The singularity and sanguinary nature of Manuel Blanco Romasanta's story hardly suffice to explain the artistic fascination with this wolf-man. Neither authors nor directors appear particularly interested in the historical, scientific, or juridical facts of the case—or even in maintaining a bit of verisimilitude for that matter. Instead, these works opt to draw on superstition, conjecture, and sensationalism for their appeal. The symbolic and creative possibilities that the werewolf offers are more important than historical accuracy. I would argue that, like other nineteenth-century monsters analyzed by Judith Halberstam, the Wolf-man of Allariz "metaphorized modern subjectivity as a balancing act between inside/outside, female/male, body/mind, native/foreign, proletarian/aristocrat."[10] I want to suggest that it is this aspect of Romasanta's story that makes it so alluring for writers and directors who want to understand Galician identity through the figure of an ambiguous, abject, and yet iconic figure. Beyond just the barbarity of the homicides—the tearing away at his victims' flesh with his hands and mouth—, Romasanta's crimes cross gendered, sexual, and national boundaries and allow us to reconsider the relationship between regional and sexual identity in Galicia.

Despite their theoretical richness and complexity, monstrous bodies— and Gothic and horror literature and film in general—have traditionally been under-analyzed in Iberian studies. Over the last few years there has been an attempt to appraise the cultural and political value that these works hold. Throughout the twentieth century, these genres were considered an affront to the standards of good taste, "a rejection of 'accepted' critical criteria."[11] The commercial and critical acclaim they have now received is reason to assert along with Andrew Willis that "Spanish horror has now truly moved from the margins to the mainstream."[12] This is true also of literary studies, which are seeing an increased interest in the Gothic.[13] In an analysis of B-genres in Spain from 1939 to the present, almost the same period that these works on Romasanta span (1947-2004), Tatjana Pavlović explores some general aspects about these genres that are worth considering when approaching these works on the werewolf. In particular, Pavlović reminds us that "human bodies are not merely natural, biological entities; they are penetrated by culture through and through. The actions and representations of bodies are regulated and controlled by dominant power structures, but these same bodies can also be appropriated by subcultures and put to divergent and oppositional uses."[14] The real human body of Manuel Romasanta is one that was also traversed by medical, cultural, and legal discourses in the nineteenth century so that, despite our own disbelief in werewolves, his lycanthropy became quite literally a legal and medical matter of fact. That historical body, subjected to State power and interrogation, has been used in different periods by authors to both support and question the hegemonic relationships between nation, gender, and sexuality.

Before analyzing the novels and films, I would like to briefly review the historical case of Romasanta as detailed by anthropologist and biographer Mariño-Ferro in order to understand how the lycanthrope's body was written into nineteenth-century history as a queer, regional, and monstrous subjectivity. Manuel Blanco Romasanta was born in 1809 in Esgos, an impoverished village in Ourense. Mariño Ferro points out that Romasanta was written into the registry and baptismal records as a female by the name of Manuela; it is not until his confirmation that he appears as Manuel. Believing Romasanta to have suffered from a genetic or glandular condition or a type a hermaphroditism, Mariño-Ferro argues that the apparition of masculine secondary sexual traits at the onset of puberty would have played a fundamental role in the psychological disorders Romasanta would develop as an adult. While I am hesitant to establish such a clear relationship of causality between sexual ambiguity and criminality, it is worth noting that this curious circumstance (perhaps unknown to the writers and directors) is not explicitly mentioned in any of the novels or films. Nevertheless, issues of gender and sexual ambiguity seep into the fiction —for example, Benito's apparent asexuality in *El bosque del lobo* or Manuel's homoerotic attractions to men or effeminate behaviour in Conde's *Romasanta*. Also, the very Gothic/horror genre is one that plays with bodily and gender ambiguity. Echoing theorist James Elkins, Pavlović argues that these types of films depend upon our desire to protect bodies and keep them whole at the same time as they obsess over the ability to tear away the skin and reveal the inside.[15] This is true of the Romasanta stories, where on the one hand there is a desire to keep the victims intact and safe, but at the same time there is excitement and thrill in those moments of transformation when Romasanta tears away his clothes, a common trope in werewolf folktales that is symbolic of the shedding of the skin to reveal the animal's body,[16] or the desire to expose a hidden truth that we find in each of these works. This particular tension between female victims and the male killer also forces the reader/viewer into a position of gender ambiguity. Carol Clover, in *Men, Women and Chain Saws* (1992), a seminal work on gender in the horror film, has shown that these films allow the viewer to adopt different gendered points of view, identify alternatively with the protagonist (masculine) monster and the vulnerable (female) victim.[17] This is probably most notable in the *Romasanta* novel and film in which the reader/viewer's initial identification with Manuel—in the book the narrator/protagonist and in the film the family's seeming protector—shifts by the works' ends almost entirely to Bárbara, the female heroine who brings Romasanta to justice. Even though the sexual and gender ambiguity of the historical Romasanta are not explicitly perceived by these writers and directors as necessarily being the cause of the criminality, ambiguity is certainly characteristic of the wolf-man's monstrosity and perversity and of the way the stories themselves are structured.

Returning to the historical case, accusations that Romasanta was a murderer began to circulate as early as the 1830s and 1840s with claims that he'd murdered the former servant of a church superior and, later, a constable in León. The modern, fictionalized versions omit the murders of any males, representing, instead, only female victims.[18] This decision by authors and directors explicitly genders and sexualizes the crimes, which also problematically reproduces the identification with femininity and victimization. Romasanta was never convicted but returned to Galicia where he ingratiated himself with many of the local peasants, aristocrats, and clergymen.

Character references gathered from locals, as Mariño-Ferro reveals, seem quite consistent in describing Romasanta as amiable, devout, sensible, and prudent, only showing reserve about his effeminate behaviour and labour in traditionally feminine chores. Romasanta dabbled in a range of occupations—servant, farmer, tailor, cook but principally as a travelling salesman, a career quite common in those parts given the proximity to Portugal and Castile, which would allow for easier access to goods which could then be brought back to Galicia and sold.

His benign presence and non-threatening sexuality made Manuel a seemingly safe guide for poor Galicians who needed to be led across the border in search of work. Manuel managed to convince at least three townswomen—all single mothers of illegitimate children—to sell their belongings and head to Santander in search of well-paid work. Rather than conducting them safely through the woods, he would murder them and their young children, taking their money and clothing to sell. Both the real and fictitious female victims are women considered sexually promiscuous, one of traditional conventions of horror film.[19] Conde and Plaza avoid the moralistic pitfall of that tradition by having Bárbara, the sister of the victims who avenges their deaths, also be sexually active.

The victims' family members made official accusations against Romasanta, but he was defended by the priest with whom he lived (Mariño-Ferro goes so far as to insinuate that their relationship may have been sexual) and other wealthy benefactors. Incriminating evidence piled up against him and he was ultimately detained and brought to justice in Allariz. Manuel admitted to the murders but argued he was not to blame, claiming he murdered the women because of an ancestral curse that turned him into a werewolf. It is unclear if Romasanta claimed to be a werewolf in an attempt to appeal to Galician folklore and superstition in order find believers of his tale, or if he was playing mad to get out of the death penalty, or if he truly did suffer a form of psychosis. The forensic and medical teams, by the standards of the day, were unable to detect any psychological abnormalities.

Manuel was subsequently sentenced to death by the local authorities whereupon his case was again heard in A Coruña to the same result. The idea that there was a lycanthrope in Galicia attracted the attention of a Mr. Philips, an electro-biologist working in Algeria. As a result of his intervention in the case, the government of Isabel II commuted the sentence to lifelong imprisonment.

The story of Romasanta, as Mariño-Ferro points out, provides a window into a number of aspects of life in the nineteenth century: "A crónica do home lobo Romasanta é un dramático documento sobre a cara oculta da especie humana e un bo retrato da sociedade do seu tempo, con datos sobre vida cotiá, economía, vestimenta, medicina, administración de xustiza e, por suposto, sobre determinadas crenzas tradicionais. Podería considerarse un episodio, moi destacado, do longo enfrontamento entre tradición e modernidade."[20] Despite this historical richness, Martínez-Barbeito, Conde, Olea, and Plaza appear less interested in creating historical period pieces, and find in the story of Romasanta the makings of Gothic narratives. The epigraphs and prologues to the novels, interestingly, both claim to be written accounts of oral histories handed down from paternal figures—Martínez-Barbeito's father and Conde's grandfather. As such, these works introduce, to borrow from Sánchez-Ferraces's work on Risco's werewolf fiction, "algunhas crenzas e tradicións que, fluíndo permanentemente pola memoria colectiva dunha comunidade, religan a quen as cre ou practica a unha visión máxica do mundo sitemáticamente acosada pola racionalidade da vida moderna."[21] These fictionalized histories and their filmic adaptations blur boundaries between oral history and literature, tradition and modernity, and truth and fiction, generating the "disruption of realism and all generic purity" that Halberstam considers characteristic of horror.[22] Both writers call attention to the artifice of their works at the same time as they claim them to be true. Martínez-Barbeito gives Romasanta a new name (Benito Freire) and Conde —who in the introduction to his first-person pseudo-autobiography by Romasanta claims "Esta historia é certa" [this story is certain][23]— suggests quite the opposite in the novel's subtitle, "memorias incertas do home lobo," or "uncertain memoirs of the Wolf-Man." The film version of *Romasanta* takes even more literary and cinematographic liberties than does the novel such as the introduction of another lycanthrope, the introduction of a fearless heroine, and a scene of transformation into a werewolf. Nevertheless, in their fictions these writers and directors do evidence the tensions between tradition and modernity that the original nineteenth-century tales sought to exemplify.

The werewolf confronts us with a primitive and abject subjectivity, a man who would appear to emerge from the world of folktales as an affront to modern history and identity.

The novel *El bosque de Ancinces* as well as the film *El bosque del lobo* are revealing when their production is considered within their historic context. The representation of werewolves in Spanish cultural production was a contentious issue during Franco's rule. Carlos Aguilar and Antonio Lázaro-Reboll both show how censors placed heavy restrictions on the genre. Aguilar, for example, states that "el Terror español de entonces tanto cuidaba obvias cuestiones geográfico-argumentales (la acción transcurría fuera de España, los argumentos versaban sobre arquetipos universales, los lugares de rodaje eran insólitos) como desplegaba recursos más sutiles, sobre todo en cuanto al reparto: los intérpretes estaban doblados (así el espectador común del país no identificaba las voces con las de filmes españoles de otros géneros) y, además, solían ser o bien directamente extranjeros...o bien españoles que trabajaban poco o nada fuera del género."[24] Great pains were taken to project the werewolf beyond Spain. The same can be said during the nineteenth century when the government worked to keep the story out of the news and to resolve the case as speedily as possible to avoid public scandal. Scholars and critics who have studied the Spanish werewolves movies, most notably the Naschy cult classics, typically find a series of poorly funded B-films, with flat story lines, gratuitous sex and nudity, and less than impressive special effects.[25] Although the werewolf genre has been erased from the Spanish cinematic canon, as Lázaro-Reboll points out, these films bear witness to "the international and transcultural dimension of Spanish horror." [26]Something of that transcultural tradition still remains. As the story has moved between literary and cinematic genres, it has also crossed linguistic lines, most notably seen in the move from *Romasanta. Memorias incertas do home lobo* to *Romasanta: The Werewolf Hunt.*

The Galician werewolf stories represented by Martínez-Barbeito and Olea are exceptions to the abovementioned trends that defined the werewolf genre during Francoism. The gore, sexuality, and foreignness of a film like *La noche de Walpurgis* (1970) are completely absent from Pedro Olea's *El bosque del lobo*, produced the same year. Unlike other werewolf movies of the time, Olea's werewolf is recorded in Castilian and played by a recognizable Spanish actor, the filming locations and settings are identified as Galicia and Castile, and the bloody spectacle is left to the imagination. The Galician werewolf, unlike other Spanish werewolves, is undeniably a domestic product. Even the novel by Martínez-Barbeito upon which the film is based is ensconced in Galicia's geography and culture, containing lengthy passages describing landscape, funeral rites, marketplaces, superstitions, and celebrations. In *El bosque de Ancines* the Galician characters are determined by their environment: "Pero por doquier se agolpaba la niebla, que empapaba los cuerpos y parecía sumir a los espíritus en un mundo irreal poblado de seres fantásticos...trasgos y almas en pena."[27] Both authors and directors alike draw heavily on Galician folklore for the more fictitious aspects of the work, particularly those myths about the last male child in a long line of males being a werewolf, and other particulars about the process of transformation such as eating dirt or rolling around in it, which we see the protagonist do in *El bosque del lobo*. In earlier works about Romasanta, as Alfredo Conde points out, the werewolf is "presentado como un galego ignorante e supersticioso, degradado e inculto, que se creu atinxido dunha maldición que certamente respondía a sentires ancestrais."[28] In Martínez-Barbeito and Olea's works, the lycanthropy is not the problem of an individual but is instead a product and proof of Galicia's backwardness, a primitiveness that is embodied by the werewolf. There are also lengthy passages in which townspeople tell tales of lycanthropy which read as tales of Galician, rural backwardness. To this degree, these two works are like the works by Risco and Piñeiro insofar as they establish an over-simplified relation between the traditional, primitive and Galician, similar to the type of representations of Galicia that flourished during the end of the twentieth century and that critics such as María Reimóndez have criticized as a form of traditionalism that leads to a cultural "autocompracencia esencialista" ("essentialist complacency") that stifles more political and modernizing impulses within the culture.[29]

But the Galician werewolf story can also challenge essentialist notions of Galician identity, as the four works being analyzed also do. Even though the Galician werewolf is steeped in its locality and continually reminds us that we are in Spain, we can also argue that it simultaneously helps establish an idea of Galicia as a foreign territory within Spain, at once under Spanish jurisdiction but culturally distinct. The border is a necessary space and constant element in each re-telling of the Galician werewolf story. The repeated references to the border remind us that Galicia's connection with the rest of Spain is not seamless. The wolf-man continually slips back and forth across borders. The fact that Romasanta was a travelling salesman is integrated into each of the modern versions and is necessary for the Gothic tale. Again, all of the fictitious versions incorporate the fact that Romasanta was a traveling salesman and guide. This fact makes him into a wanderer, one of the stock characters of the horror genre who generates fear because he represents the collapsing of boundaries, blurring distinctions between insides and outsides, which is the very essence of the genre.

As folkloric and essentialist as the Galician werewolf may appear to be, we are also unsatisfied to think of him as a positive image of Galician masculinity or as being entirely Galician. In these four fictitious representations of the Romasanta story, his victims are poor Galician emigrant women in search of work. He preys on these marginalized figures adding to the marginalization and victimization that they were forced to deal with as Galicians in the nineteenth century. In Martínez-Barbeito and Olea's works, Romasanta's victims are convinced to make the trip after being regaled with gifts and stories from beyond Galicia. As Martínez-Barbeito writes, "Las aldeanas se sentían deslumbradas por el brillo de las peinetas y los broches y casi tanto por la labia de Benito, que no paraba de contarles maravillas de los lugares por donde había pasado."[30] In many ways Romasanta is less representative of Galicia and seeks to identify with the Spanish centrist state that was draining the region of resources and its workforce. In Conde's novel, Romasanta is quite explicitly the anti-Galician. Even though Romasanta comes from the same class and region as the emigrant workers and also earns his living by travelling back and forth to Castile, he tries desperately to separate himself from the Galician laborers. He takes great pains as a young boy to master speaking and writing Castilian to set himself socially above the people around him; later, while working as a guide to the emigrants, he despises them and their plight, at one point saying "Molestábame velos e gustaba de me saber distinto deles, liberado do seu xugo."[31] If the monster can signify myriad and contradictory ideas, Romasanta is simultaneously representative of both Spain and Galicia, and criminally traverses the border between them. The relationship between the werewolf's monstrosity and disruption of national borders is perhaps best illustrated in Martínez-Barbeito's novel when the protagonist, fleeing from the authorities, temporarily takes up residence in Couto Mixto, where "no reconocían potestad alguna de las dos Monarquías peninsulares y alternativamente se acogían a una o a otra según les conviniese; su estatuto de frontera favorecía el doble juego…así que no podía imaginar Benito una salida más segura y cómoda de España que la fisura que el Coto abría en la raya portuguesa."[32] The werewolf is an outsider within or, in Agamben's language, represents an included exclusion or threshold. The Galician werewolf, like Agamben's werewolf, is "a zone of indistinction and continuous transition between man and beast, nature and culture,"[33] a figure "that dwells paradoxically in both while belonging to neither."[34] This is perhaps also reinforced by the jurisdiction in the case that will ultimately decide not to punish him, but also not fully pardon him either.

Another constant in the different versions of Romasanta's story is his problematic sexuality. Here is where we encounter a much wider range of inconsistency among the different tales, even in the adaptations from book to film. In the 1947 novel *El bosque de Ancines* the werewolf is described as being hairy, with a wide face, high cheekbones, a strong jaw, and pointed teeth.[35] He is generally found to be attractive and pleasant by the women he encounters. In the towns he travels between he has different lovers. While the character doesn't suffer from any mental disorders of which we know, his attacks on his victims are preceded by attacks of epilepsy that the characters believe to be a curse rather than an illness. The seductive salesman's masculinity and heterosexuality are amplified during his murders. Benito strips away his clothing, gets on all fours, and attacks his victims. The violent acts usually combine murder with sexual violation and titillation: "Luego de un brusco saltó, se alabanzó sobre la mujer, que yacía sin sentido, la estranguló con sus dedos crispados y le clavó una y otra vez los agudos colmillos en el cuello hasta que brotó la sangre a borbotones calientes…ayudándose con los dientes y las duras uñas, desgarró los tejidos, cortó las venas, arrancó los nervios y los cartílagos y lamió, lamió ávidamente, la humedad que había en ellas."[36] Later in the novel he kills an old woman, afterwards he removes her clothing: "Al verla desnuda, hecha un espantajo grotesco, arrugada la piel y fláccidas las carnes, se rió; la abrió de piernas y volvió a reír."[37] The novel typifies the violence and moral depravity of the *tremendismo* of the Spanish novel during the period, meant to reinforce the dominant, conservative moral code. Benito's is a masculinity and heterosexuality run rampant that goes to the point of devouring women. There are men who almost become his victims but manage to escape. Benito's murdering of only women establishes the traditional, misogynistic division of male/aggressor versus female/victim so commonly found in horror films and makes his crimes appear sexual in nature; however, that masculinity and heterosexuality are called into question by his inability or unwillingness to kill males, either because of an impotence (as is the case with the other traveling salesman) or affection (his decision to not kill the adolescent boy Mingos, whose admiration of Benito in the book leads him to claim to be a lycanthrope as well).

Interestingly, when the film adaptation was made in 1970, the hypersexuality of the werewolf and the graphic descriptions of the attack scenes were lost. The protagonist of the film is short, unkempt, and almost offensively unattractive. Far from the ladies' man he is in the novel, the film's wolf-man seems socially awkward, timid and servile, making his transformation into a murderer all the more shocking. Not only is there no allusion to rape or any sexual gratification in the scenes of violence, the film alludes to the character having experienced a sexual trauma as a child. The film opens with a scene of two older boys holding down a young Benito, forcing him to watch the breeding of two horses. That scene, together with other flashbacks from his youth, seems to offer an explanation of the character's queerness and asexuality throughout the rest of the film as well as his sympathy or affection for Mingos.

Conde's Romasanta is described as being small in stature and as having boyish good looks. He attracts women and has a number of lovers that he sleeps with while the emigrant men are away working. Conde's werewolf, while not having any relationships with men, does often express admiration for handsome men, occasionally feeling "un calafrío estraño" ("a strange chill") upon looking at them.[38] Like the historical figure, Conde's Romasanta engages in activities typically considered feminine such as cooking and weaving. He is a self-declared exhibitionist and has a fascination with being seen, a trait he himself considers feminine. Like the werewolf in *El bosque de Ancines* and of many of the European werewolf legends, Conde's werewolf sheds his clothing before killing his victims; however, he does this not out of impulse but to keep his clothes clean. Given his exhibitionist tendencies, these moments are ones of sexual power and pleasure. As the protagonist says, "debo recoñecer que o feito de me ver espido diante da aínda cálida nudez deles [das miñas vítimas], fosen homes ou mulleres, novos ou vellos, dotábame da enerxía e do quentor abondos, do valor necesario, para levar a termo calquera ocorrencia que me viñera ós miolos."[39] This queerness is written out of the film version. The film's Romasanta, played by British actor Julian Sands, unlike the one in the novel, is a tall, muscular womanizer whose gender and sexuality correspond to dominant models of masculinity. As sexual and attractive as he is portrayed to be, the only shot of Sand's naked body which occurs during a scene of transformation is monstrous and animalistic: Manuel is lying on the floor in a fetal position as rain washes clumps of wolf hair and mud from his body. So, if in the novel the male body is a desirable body, or one that is at least desired by Romasanta in the novel as a masculine one, the only sexualized body on display in the film is that of actress Elsa Pataky, who plays Bárbara, and as such the camera sets a more heterosexual, masculine gaze on the female body than does the book.

By way of conclusion, I want to look at the endings of the works in which this predatory and abnormal masculinity is put on trial. Halberstam again reminds us that even though the Gothic monster can represent a queer sexuality, the works are not always subversive and often reinforce hegemonic subjectivities: "Gothic fiction is a technology of subjectivity, on which produces the deviant subjectivities opposite which the normal, the healthy, and the pure can be known."[40] *El bosque de Ancines* finds the fault for Romasanta's actions in Galicia—its landscape, backwardness, superstitions, and traditions. As the lawyer declares, "La culpa es de la ignorancia del pueblo; háganse muchas escuelas y se cerrarán muchas prisiones."[41] The townspeople are gullible enough to believe that Benito is a real werewolf, and the aristocracy—represented here as a bunch of rich women with feminist inclinations à la Concepción Arenal—attempt to have Benito pardoned, arguing that he just needs rehabilitation and that prison or death would be too cruel a sentence. Luckily, the Spanish crown remains steadfast in its decision and the death penalty is administered, the anomalous masculinity is destroyed, and order is restored. This is hardly a surprising conclusion given the time period. The film, however, elides the court proceedings, so rather than seeing a Spanish court have to deal with a throng of backward, superstitious Galicians, the film opts to have the townspeople hunt and kill Benito. Justice is still imparted but in this representation it is the Galician people that have triumphed over the queer, primitive monster.

Conde's *Romasanta* is a vindication of the Galician people who know that Romasanta is lying and deserves to be executed. The Spanish authorities and shortsighted medical teams entertain the fact that Romasanta could in fact be a lycanthrope. As Conde states in the introduction, "os máis supersticiosos e incultos non foron nin a xente da aldea nin a clase médica ou forense galega, senón...maiormente a clase científica foránea, a prensa da época e máis todos aqueles que, dentro e fóra dos nosos lindes, aceptaron presentar a Manuel Blanco Romasanta dediante do mundo como un home lobo real."[42] In fact, in the novel, Romasanta only becomes "o home lobo" when the Spanish get hold of him. As the Galician people show up to the courthouse to heckle the prisoner; Romasanta says: "Reprocháronme a berros que vendera unto de cristián e que me excedera nas miñas ganancias para que as señoritangas portuguesas lavaran as súas partes máis pudendas, chamáronme ladrón ou maricallo, pero nunca home lobo."[43] The Galician werewolf is not then a product of Galician folklore but a Spanish invention. This monstrous creation also allows the Spanish crown to pardon Romasanta, becoming another injustice to be suffered by the Galician people.

In the film based on this novel, there is a more cinematic twist, and rural Galician femininity triumphs over both Romasanta and the Spanish judicial system. Upon hearing about the pardon, Bárbara, the sister of one of the victims and former lover of Manuel's, arrives at the prison and murders the killer. Through the fictitious figure of Bárbara, the film introduces another stock character of horror film that Clover has referred to as the "final girl,"[44] the character who "alone looks death in the face, but she alone also finds the strength either to stay the killer long enough to be rescued... or to kill him herself."[45] Of the final girl, Clover writes: "Just as the killer is not fully masculine, she is not fully feminine."[46] In *Romasanta*, Bárbara goes from being afraid to look at the mutilated bodies found in the woods by police to acquiring a knife, a phallic weapon, and turns the hunter into the hunted. The film can thus be seen as the triumph of a Galician and feminist figure over that of a predatory, masculine monster that is a creation of Spanish authorities and myths of Galician primitivism.

"The monster," as Halberstam again reminds us, "always represents the disruption of categories, the destruction of boundaries, and the presence of impurities and so we need monsters and we need to recognize and celebrate our own monstrosities."[47] Despite the werewolf containing such a negative image of masculinity or Galicianness, he is necessary insofar as he embodies a threat to hegemonic notions of masculinity in Spain and awakens a sense of thrill as he questions national, sexual, and gendered limitations. The Gothic, as Sedgwick has argued, is able to "open horizons beyond social patters, rational decisions, and institutionally approved emotions; in a word, to enlarge the sense of reality and its impact on the human being."[48] Within a Galician context, the werewolf questions assumptions about national and sexual identity and, in Sedgwick's terminology, creates "a doubleness where singleness should be."[49] Galician literary criticism has marked a tension between the need to explore Galicianness and a desire to move beyond it. The value of Galician literature has traditionally been determined by nationalistic, sexist, and linguistic criteria but, as Helena Miguélez-

Carballeira has argued, there is an increasing need for an alternative understanding of a Galician narrative as a "constantly transforming entity (not only in size and quality, which is the premise of the nationalist take on it), transfigured by variously defined peoples and languages (not just the Galician language) and, most emphatically, through a historically fluctuating system of values."[50] The Romasanta stories offer just that: a tale that is traversed by Galician history, politics, and culture but that is transformative, shifting, and unrestricted to any particular ideology or language.

In each of these twentieth-century depictions, Romasanta's lycanthropy and his aberrant masculinity are entrenched in ideas about Galicianness and male sexuality. Precisely what each work suggests about these, however, varies between each account. As we can see in these four works on Romasanta, the werewolf becomes a symbol that can embody multiple and contradictory notions. The Galician wolf-man can represent both a threat to the notion of a modern, hegemonic, Spanish masculine identity (Conde's *Romasanta*, for example) as well as evidence of a Galician alterity and queerness (*El bosque de Ancines* or *El bosque del lobo*). To this effect, Halberstam reminds us: "The monster's body indeed, is a machine that, in its Gothic mode, produces meaning and can represent any horrible trait that the reader feeds into the narrative. The monster functions as monster, in other words, when it is able to condense as many fear-producing traits as possible into one body."[51] The werewolf's body and his crimes disrupt notions of national, gender, and sexual purity or stability. Romasanta is simultaneously animal and human, historical and fictitious, hyper-masculine and effeminate, heterosexual and queer, a Galician and a foreigner, traditional and modern, mentally and physically infirm as well as physically strong and criminally cunning, protagonist and villain.

This hybridity and duality is not limited to the wolf-man but is, as cultural critics and historians have shown, characteristic of modern Galician identity.[52] In Galicia, as José Colmeiro states, "apparently opposing cultural forces create new hybrid realities with new forms of identity that bind the old with the new, the local with the global."[53] Within such a contex, the wolf-man becomes a privileged representative of such an identity, and embodiment of duality and opposition through which we can engage with a number of cultural tensions. The werewolf calls attention to cultural tensions, as well as questions binaries, boundaries and identities but rarely does it offer satisfactory resolutions, questioning the difference between the "other" and the "self." José B. Monleón's statement, in his study of the Gothic and fantastic in eighteenth- and nineteenth-century Spain, is quite relevant in any discussion of Romasanta: "This definite internalization of otherness, this final inclusion of unreason within the parameters of reason, implied not only that monstrosity was "real," but that it actually formed part of reason. The monsters were possible because "we" were the monsters."[54] Romasanta, a marginal figure from the nineteenth century, continually resurfaces over the course of the twentieth century in a different languages and media and ideological contexts, but always with the intention of raising questions about ambiguous national and sexual identity in Galicia and Spain.

Notes

[1]   Garrosa-Gude, "Unha inquietante," 132. "The region of Spain in which the legends and oral stories about lycanthropes had, perhaps, the most popular circulation and an incorporation into highbrow literary works that granted it an even more ample diffusion" (This and all subsequent translations from Galician into English are mine). A similar argument was made earlier in the century by Vicente Risco, who argued the prominent position it occupies: "da al lobo una categoría estética que lo hace digno de figurar en pie de igualdad por lo menos, entre los personajes fundamentales de nuestra épica popular y literaria" (Risco, "Un caso," 226), that is, "gives the wolf an aesthetic category that makes it worthy of figuring on equal footing at least, among the foundational characters of our popular and literary epic."

[2]   Vaz da Silva, "Iberian."

[3]   Risco, ibid., 776-783; Mariño-Ferro, *Lobos*.

[4]   Risco, ibid., 795. "The myth of the wolf-man is an honorable part of our clean blazon."

[5]   Sánchez-Ferraces, "Vicente," 112.

[6]   Alfonso R. Castelao, for example, advocated a new Galician coat of arms that would replace the Catholic chalice and Eucharist with a more communist sickle-wielding mermaid: "E a sirea, que perteñece â heráldica galega, como símbolo mariño que fale do engado atlántico, orixe das nosas aventuras" (Castelao, "Os novos," 2), that is, "The mermaid, who belongs to Galician heraldry, as a maritime symbol that speaks of the Atlantic mystique, that is the origin of our adventures."

[7]   I am very grateful to Jaume Martí-Olivella for bringing this film to my attention at the "Beyond Don Juan: Rethinking Iberian Masculinities" conference held in NYU in March-April 2011, where this paper was originally presented, and for our subsequent conversation on Piñeiro's use of the werewolf in his film.

[8]   A rather complete annotated bibliography of the fiction and non-fiction dealing with Romasanta can be found in Castro-Vicente, "Un prego."

[9]   Mariño-Ferro, ibid., 13.

[10]   Halberstam, *Skin*, 1995.

[11]   Willis, "From the Margins," 240.

[12]   Ibid., 248.

[13]   Six, *Gothic*.

[14]   Pavlović, *Despotic*, 4.

[15]   Ibid., 140.

[16]   Vaz da Silva, ibid.

[17]   Clover, *Men*, 45.

18   If male victims are mentioned at all it is usually only as a passing mention by Romasanta or in the list of charges brought against Romasanta in the scenes dealing with the court proceedings.

19   Clover, ibid., 32-35.

20   Mariño-Ferro, *Manuel(a)*, 13. "The chronicle of the wolf-man Romasanta is a dramatic document about the hidden face of the human species and a good representation of the society of times, with details about daily life, economy, clothing, medicine, the administering of justice, and, of course, about certain traditional beliefs. It could be considered an episode illustrative of the long struggle between tradition and modernity."

21   Sánchez-Ferraces, ibid., 111. "Some beliefs and traditions that, flowing permanently through the collective memory of a community, relegates those who believe or practice them to a magical vision of the world systematically under attack by the rationality of modern life."

22   Halberstam, ibid., 11.

23   Conde, *Romasanta*, 9.

24   Aguilar, *Cine*, 24. English translation in Lázaro-Reboll, "La noche," 13: "Spanish horror took care of obvious geographical and narrative questions (the action was set outside Spain, the story-lines dealt with universal archetypes, the shooting locations were unusual)...the actors were dubbed...and they used to be either foreign or Spanish who did not work –or hardly worked– outside the genre."

25   Díaz-Maroto, *Los hombres lobo*, 46-67.

26   Lázaro-Reboll, ibid., 129.

27   Martínez-Barbeito, *El bosque*, 60. "But everywhere there had accumulated a fog that drenched the bodies and seemed to plunge the spirits in an unreal world inhabited by fantastic beings...mischief makers and penitent souls."

28   Conde, ibid., 12: "is presented as an ignorant and superstitious, degraded and uncultured Galician, who believed himself afflicted by a curse that really corresponded to ancestral views."

29   Reimóndez, "Whose Heritage," 194.

30   Martínez-Barbeito, ibid., 59: "The townswomen were dazzled by the shine of the combs and brooches and almost as much by the loquacity of Benito, who ceaselessly related the wonders of the places through which he had passed."

31   Conde, ibid., 26: "It bothered me to see them and I liked to know that I was different from them, free from their yoke."

32   Martínez-Barbeito, ibid., 98: "they didn't recognize the sovereignty of either of the two peninsular monarchies and alternatively adhered to one or the other depending how it could be beneficial; its status a border favored this double game...so that Benito couldn't imagine a more suitable and safe exit from Spain the fissure that the Couto opened along the dividing line with Portugal."

33   Agamben, *Homo Sacer*, 109.

34   Ibid., 105.

35   Martínez-Barbeito, ibid., 9.

36   Ibid., 21: "Then after an abrupt leap, he balanced atop the woman, who lay unconscious, strangled her with his tense fingers and nailed in his pointy fangs into her neck over and over again until the blood came pouring out in warm gushes...making use of his teeth and hard fingernails, he tore apart the tissues, cut the veins and tore the nerves and cartilage and licked, licked avidly, the wetness that there was in them."

37   Ibid., 83: "Upon seeing her naked, looking a grotesque scarecrow, with wrinkled skin and flacid flesh, he laughed; he spread her legs and laughed again."

38   Conde, ibid., 93.

[39] Ibid., 89: "I should admit that seeing myself naked before the still warm nudity of my victims, whether they were men or women, young or old, gave me the energy and fire I needed, the resolve necessary to carry out to completion any idea that would then come into my head."

[40] Halberstam, ibid., 2.

[41] Martínez-Barbeito, ibid., 161: "The blame rests with the people's ignorance; build many schools and many prisions will close."

[42] Conde, ibid., 12-13: "The most superstitious and uneducated where the common folk, nor the judges and medical authorities of Galicia, but rather it was mostly the foreign scientists, the press of the era, that within and beyond our natural border presented Manuel Blanco Romasanta as a real wolf-man."

[43] Ibid., 94: "They shouted reproaches that I had sold human fat, that I had made excessive wealth so that young Portuguese ladies could wash their most private parts, they called me thief or faggot, but never Wolf-Man."

[44] Clover, ibid., 35-41.

[45] Ibid., 35.

[46] Ibid., 40.

[47] Halberstam, ibid., 27.

[48] Sedgwick, *Coherence*, 3.

[49] Ibid., 13.

[50] Miguélez-Carballeira, "Alternative Values," 281.

[51] Halberstam, ibid., 21.

[52] Colmeiro, "Peripheral Visions;" Hooper, "Galicia desde Londres;" Toro, "Bagpipes."

[53] Colmeiro, ibid., 217.

[54] Monleón, *A Specter*, 171.

Bibliography

Agamben, Giorgio. *Homo Sacer: Sovereign Power and Bare Life*, translated by Daniel Heller-Roazen. Stanford: Stanford University Press, 1998.

Aguilar, Carlos. *Cine fantástico y de terror español*. San Sebastian: Donostia Kultura, 1999.

El bosque del lobo. DVD. Directed by Pedro Olea. 1970. Madrid: Divisa Home Video, 2007.

Castelao, Alfonso R. "Os novos símbolos da Nova Galiza." *Nova Galiza. Boletin Quincenal dos Escritores Galegos Antifeixistes* 6 (1936): 2.

Castro-Vicente, Félix Francisco. "Un prego de cordel descoñecido sobre o caso de Manuel Blanco Romasanta: o 'home do unto' e unha escolma bibliográfica sobre o mesmo." *Lethes: Cadernos Cuturais do Limia* (2007-8): 79-94.

Clover, Carol J. *Men, Women, and Chain Saws: Gender in the Modern Horror Film*. Princeton: Princeton University Press, 1992.

Colmeiro, José F. "Peripheral Visions, Global Positions: Remapping Galician Culture." *Bulletin of Hispanic Studies* 86, no. 2 (2009): 213-230.

Conde, Alfredo. *Romasanta. Memorias incertas do home lobo*. Santiago de Compostela: Sotelo Blanco Edicións, 2004.

Díaz-Maroto, Carlos. *Los hombres lobo en el cine. Licántropos y otros hombres bestia en la pantalla*. Madrid: Ediciones Jaguar, 2004.

Garrosa-Gude, José Luis. "Unha inquietante presenza: lobos e lobishomes no imaginario galego e universal." In *O mito que fascina: do lobo ao lobishome. Actas das II xornadas de literatura de tradición oral*, edited by Isidoro Novo and Antonio Reigosa, 113-143. A Coruña: Asociación de Escritores en Lingua Galega, 2009.

Halberstam, Judith. *Skin Shows: Gothic Horror and the Technology of Monsters*. Durham, NC: Duke University Press, 1995.

Hooper, Kirsty. "Galicia desde Londres desde Galicia: New Voices in the 21-century Diaspora." *Journal of Spanish Cultural Studies* 7, no 2 (2006): 171-188.

Lázaro-Reboll, Antonio. "*La noche de Walpurgis/Shadow of the Werewolf. León Klimovsky, 1970.*" In *The Cinema of Spain and Portugal*, edited by Alberto Mira, 129-136. New York: Wallflower Press, 2005.

Mariño-Ferro, Xosé Ramón. *Lobos, lobas e lobishomes*. Vigo: Edicións do Cumio, 1997.

———. *Manuel(a) Branco Romasanta, o lobishome asasino*. Vigo: Nigratrea, 2007.

Martínez-Barbeito, Carlos. *El bosque de Ancines*. 2nd ed. Barcelona: Ediciones Destino, 1966.

Miguélez-Carballeira, Helena. "Alternative Values: From the National to the Sentimental in the Redrawing of Galician Literary History." *Bulletin of Hispanic Studies* 86, no 2 (2009): 271-292.

Monleón, José B. *A Specter is Haunting Europe: A Sociohistorical Approach to the Fantastic*. Princeton: Princeton University Press, 1990.

Pavlović, Tatjana. *Despotic Bodies and Transgressive Bodies: Spanish Culture from Francisco Franco to Jesús Franco*. New York: SUNY Press, 2003.

———. "Gender and Spanish Horror Film." In *Gender and Spanish Cinema*, Eds. Steven Marsh and Parvati Nair, 135-150. New York: Berg, 2004.

Pérez-López, David. *Os foxos do lobo: a caza do lobo na cultura popular*. A Coruña: Canela, 2010.

Piñeiro, Chano. *Mamasunción*. Luciano Piñeiro Producidós Cinematográficos, 1984. Film.

Reimóndez, María. "Whose Heritage Is It, Anyway? Cultural Planning and Practice in Contemporary Galicia." In *Contemporary Galician Cultural Studies: Between the Local and the Global*, edited by Kirsty Hooper and Manuel Puga Moruxa, 190-201. New York: Modern Language Association, 2011.

Risco, Vicente. "Un caso de licantropía. O home lobo." In *Obras completas*, 5, 768-795. Vigo: Galaxia, 1994.

———. "Mito y estética del lobo en Galicia." In *Obras completas*, 5, 224-226. Vigo: Galaxia, 1994.

Romasanta: The Werewolf Hunt. DVD. Directed by Paco Plaza. 2004. Lions Gate Films Home Entertainment, 2005.

Sánchez-Ferraces, Xosé Luis. "Vicente Risco e a modernidade. Lectura e análise de tres relatos. (II)." *Madrygal* 12 (2009): 109-117.

Sedgwick, Eve Kosofsky. *The Coherence of Gothic Conventions*. New York: Routledge, 1975.

Six, Abigail Lee. *Gothic Terrors: Incarceration, Duplication and Bloodlust in Spanish Narrative*. Lewisburg, PA: Bucknell University Press, 2010.

Toro, Xelís de. "Bagpipes and Digital Music: The Remixing of Galician Identity." In *Constructing Identity in Contemporary Spain: Theoretical Debates and Cultural Practice*, edited by Jo Labanyi, 237-254. New York: Oxford University Press, 2002.

Vaz da Silva, Francisco. "Iberian Seventh-Born Children, Werewolves, and the Dragon Slayer: A Case Study in the Comparative Interpretation of Symbolic Praxis and Fairytales." *Folklore* 114, no 3 (2003): 335-353.

Willis, Andrew. "From the Margins to the Mainstream: Trends in Recent Spanish Horror Cinema." In *Spanish Popular Cinema*, edited by Antonio Lázaro-Reboll and Andrew Willis, 237-249. New York: Manchester University Press, 2004.

CHAPTER 4
Mikel/Ander/Tasio: Narrative Castings and Othering Masculinities in Basque Cinema

Jaume Martí-Olivella
University of New Hampshire

Casting the Other: The Peripheral Practices of Basque Cinema

> "Casting is characterization." Hitchcock pointed out. Once a role has been cast, especially with a personality star, the essence of the fictional character is already established. In a sense, stars are more "real" than other characters, which is why many people refer to a character by the actor's name, rather than by the name of the person in the story.[1]

How would Giannetti's description of the star power in the Hollywood casting system translate when dealing with a micro-cinematography, like the Basque, where the very concept of a star system may be either truly uncanny or simply non-existing? How and when does an actor become an additional narrative tool, "a medium for communicating ideas and emotions,"[2] to say it again in Giannetti's terms? In the following pages, I will try to elucidate these questions in the context of contemporary Basque cinema while reframing them within issues of gender, cultural identity, and geopolitics. Textually, my considerations will focus on two foundational films of the 1980's, Imanol Uribe's *La muerte de Mikel* (*Mikel's Death*, 1983) and Montxo Armendáriz's *Tasio* (1983), and in two of the most recent Basque films, Roberto Castón's *Ander* (*Andrew*, 2009) and José María de Orbe's *Aita* (*Father*, 2010). Arguably, one of the most interesting parallels between these two historical moments may send us again to the most paradigmatic tension when discussing any geopolitical mappings —namely, the one existing between center and periphery. In this sense, it may be worth repeating here Imanol Uribe's own words when describing the geopolitical atmosphere of cultural alliances in the early eighties:

> In the production of *La muerte de Mikel* there is a strong Catalan participation.

> No. The film was financed in three ways. On the one hand, Aiete Films, I, personally, was the second participant and the third was Esteban Alenda, as distributor, who also had a Catalan partner...There were, however, many Catalan

technicians…It was the time when we were trying to *create a peripheral cinema* and, instead of calling technicians from Madrid, we would work with those from Barcelona who seemed closer to us.[3]

That Basque-Catalan cultural and geopolitical axis suggested by Uribe in the expression "cine periférico/peripheral cinema" that I have emphasized became more complicated and richer when one considers the iconic transactions between some of those micro-cinemas' leading actors and actresses, which, in many cases, constituted true narrative castings that underlined the uncanny nature of a Basque (or a Catalan) star system. In the introductory chapter of his volume on *Stars and Masculinites in Spanish Cinema: From Banderas to Bardem*, and borrowing from Richard Dyer's and Bruce Babington's work on British stars, Chris Perriam writes:[4]

> They have a "structured polysemy" (Dyer, 92) in relation to the social themes represented in the course of their performances and in relation to the general circulation of their images, a polysemy that is enhanced by their cumulative "iconic, transtextual sameness beneath variations" (Babington, 7), and by their special and heightened range of beautiful or impossibly manly looks.[5]

This polysemy, derived from their "iconic transtextual sameness," is, in the case of the Spanish screens, both the central and the peripheral, the very basis of the series of uncanny narrative castings that I would like to briefly explore here. In fact, the reference to the Freudean "unheimlich" has often been used by Joseba Gabilondo to characterize Basque cinema in the Spanish context as a whole:[6]

> I shall argue that Basque identity and its filmic representation are uncanny in the sense that the Spanish state and its nationalist system (in which I include both Spanish and peripheral nationalism) tend to repress them. As a result, Basque identity and its visibility recur with a violence that is clearly uncanny: familiar and yet frightening.[7]

This economy of uncanny nationalist and iconic castings will be clearly at work when considering some of the most outstanding male actors (Imanol Arias, Parxi Bisquert, Karra Elejalde or Xabi Elorriaga) to appear in Basque cinema. In the case of the films *Ander* and *Aita,* however, we are faced with two essential transgressions or displacements of such an economy. Both films are played by either unprofessional or non-iconic actors and, most importantly, both films subvert or bypass two of the most entrenched gender stereotypes within Basque cinema. In "Mapping the Gendered Space of the Basque Country," Rob Stone and Helen Jones offer a succinct account of those stereotypes:

Writing on the stereotype in colonial discourse, Homi K. Bhabha maintains that there are two ways that a colonial subject may be articulated: "as a theoretical space defined by the beliefs of the collective [and as] a political place defined by the actions of the individual" (1999: 313). However, it is the polarization of these definitions which reveals the tension at the heart of the Basque Country and suggests the impossible nature of claims for one utopian nation. Many of these claims originate in the mythic notions of difference that include ideals of gender such as the female *ama lur* (the Earth Mother) and the male *gudari* (the Warrior). However, these mythic ideals have suffered from "functional overdetermination" (Bhabha: 320) and contributed to a self-defeating dogma by signifying both rallying points and impossible objectives. The *ama lur* and the *gudari* inspired as well as inhibited Basques to strive masochistically after unattainable perfection. The articulation of difference as a reason for autonomy was thereby, quite ironically, hindered by the real differences of Basque males and females from these ideals. With no decentering of these signs, there was no reworking of character types, no disaggregation of totalizing categories and no possible individuality in terms of gender and sexuality Thus was maintained a rebuttal of all notions of incompletion or fluidity which might have disturbed both the centralist, phallocentric order of the Francoist dictatorship and, ironically, the separatist, nationalist beliefs of Basque radicals, who similarly refused to recognize any link between plurality and sexual mobility.[8]

This stereotypical fixation was also confirmed by the study recently carried out by the research group ADMIRA from the University of Seville, Spain, who presented their conclusions during the "Beyond Don Juan: Rethinking Iberian Masculinities" conference (NYU, 2011), where an initial version of this paper was also read. Here is an essential part of those conclusions:[9] "As a rule, the former examples show Basque men's relationships in homosocial environments, which are, however, predominantly heteronormative."[10] In other words, most gendered self-representations in Euskadi's cinema obey what Kaja Silverman calls "the dominant fiction,"[11] or what the four editors of *Nationalisms and Sexualities*, building on the pioneering work of George Mosse and Benedict Anderson, refer to as normative formations of the nation, when they write:

> Typically represented as a passionate brotherhood, the nation finds itself compelled to distinguish its "proper" homosociality from more explicitly sexualized male-male relations, a compulsion that requires the identification, isolation, and containment of male homosexuality…[Women] are predictably enshrined as the Mother, a "trope of ideal femininity, a fantasmatic female that secures male-male arrangements and an all male history. The idealization of motherhood by the virile fraternity would seem to entail the exclusion of all non-reproductive-oriented sexualities from the discourse of the nation.[12]

That is why, as I mentioned above, films like *Ander* and *Aita* may be considered to part from the traditional embodiment of the Basque nation inasmuch as the first incorporates a homosexual story between a Basque rural worker and a Peruvian immigrant who is hired to help in the farm labors; while the second adopts the "absent/present father" figuration, one of the most emblematic in the entire Basque cinematic canon, and expands it poetically to offer a haunting metaphor of Basque cinema itself as the ghostly inhabitant of an emptied-out "house of the father." In geopolitical terms, moreover, it seems worth mentioning here that *Ander* is Roberto Castón's first feature film and that the director is himself a Galician who has been cinematically schooled in Barcelona (CECC/Catalan Center for Cinema Studies), and who currently directs the Gay and Lesbian Film Festival in Bilbao, Euskadi, where the film was first premiered. *Aita*'s director, José María de Orbe, on the other hand, is a Basque artist who studied cinema in the American Film Institute in Los Angeles and who works in Catalonia, where his film was produced. As mentioned earlier, these cultural dialogues in and from the periphery are strongly reminiscent of those described by Imanol Uribe almost thirty years ago. And yet, the cinematic practices of the two historical moments are markedly different, the latter being representations of a global economy that seems to be no longer entrapped in the traditional iconic-nationalist struggles, or, to put it more pointedly, in the Spanish nationalist idiom of reducing any peripheral differences, that is, of always casting the other in the mirror of the Self-Same. Considered from this vantage point, and despite the enormous differences in their professional registers, Imanol Arias, Patxi Bisquert, Xabier Elorriaga and Karra Elejalde all share an "othering" position in a cinematic discourse that structures itself precisely as always occupying the place of the Other. True to this uncanny economy, it will be precisely their perceived "otherness" that allows them to become familiar faces in the context of Spanish cinema at large. In fact, their paradoxical and uncanny centrality is predicated on their very (Basque) "difference," as it may be seen in this brief summary of an interview with Karra Elejalde, significantly entitled "Karra Elejalde. El más duro del cine español" ("Karra Elejalde. The Toughest Guy in Spanish Cinema"):[13]

> Alex de la Iglesia discovered him in *Acción mutante* and he has also worked with Bajo Ulloa, Medem, Uribe…His ascent belongs in the recent boom lived by Basque actors and directors, although he is not interested in nationalisms. Karra was going to be a comic actor but has become the most appreciated noble soul beast of the new filmmakers. [A not to miss interview with our most peculiar performer.][14]

Karra Elejalde is not the "most peculiar" Spanish actor just because he is the toughest. It is mostly because of his "otherness," that is, the fact that he is a

Basque actor who was born in Salinas de Leniz, a small town on the border between *Araba* and *Guipuskoa*, and into a working class family in *Euskadi*. Elejalde will, in fact, turn these very marginal origins into his most resilient sign of identity: "I like the life of the loser. I have always lived the marginal side of life. I come from a very humble social stratus and don't want to stop sharing in and drinking those waters because my origin is truly there."[15] Elejalde's ideological toughness, moreover, is compounded by his direct resistance to any attempt at reducing him into a Hollywood-like star commodity:

> I do not look for any popularity. I fear it…That's why I try not to do much television and, in interviews, try to make clear who I am, how I think, so that I do not get reduced to "fast food."[16]

In the context of this essay, moreover, Elejalde's marginality may also illustrate the paradoxical nature of Basque cinema itself if we notice the central role he achieved during the nineties, where he took part in almost every major Basque film while becoming one of the clearest instances of the "marginal male subjectivities" described by Kaja Silverman as "those which not only acknowledge but embrace castration, alterity, and specularity"[17] and, at the same time, giving life to some intratextual variations of some more or less traditional forms of normative masculinities. Thus, he would be Lucas, the proud and fated lover of the film's female co-protagonist, Cristina Irigibel (Emma Suárez) in Julio Medem's *Vacas* (*Cows*, 1992); he would appear as the grotesque figure of Manitas in Alex de la Iglesia's ferociously funny sci-fi parody *Acción mutante* (*Mutant Action*, 1993); and he would become a kind of Spanish everyman, in the male chauvinist figure of the taxi driver and *pater familias* in Medem's second feature film, *La ardilla roja* (*The Red Squirrel,* 1993). However, that same year, he would perform in the lead role as the brutal and tender psycopath in Juanma Bajo Ulloa's *La madre muerta* (*The Dead Mother*, 1993), a remarkable performance that launched his star career, which was soon followed by his roles in Imanol Uribe's *Días contados* (*Counted Days*, 1994), and, especially, as the self-debased and feminized junkie brother, in Daniel Calparsoro's impressive debut film, *Salto al vacío* (*Leap into the Void*, 1995), or as the earthly brutal force in Julio Medem's *Tierra* (*Earth*, 1996), or, finally, as the parodic rendering of the emotionally castrated son, in Bajo Ulloa's *Airbag* (1997), which definitely established him as the most familiar face in the Basque cinema of the nineties. And that is indeed another mode of the uncanny given

Elejalde's constant effort to become (in)visible, to remain in the margins, to avoid being fixated and commodified, an effort that explained his decision to go back to the itinerant theater of his origins and to try his hand at directing films himself. Elejalde's marginality and (in)visibility, as suggested earlier, may be seen as a figuration of Basque cinema itself and may explain why Chris Perriam dismisses his potential as a Spanish male icon: "Karra Elejalde is another marginal case, an actor of some presence …who is relegated here because of the predominance of supporting, if very striking roles, rather than in co- and lead position."[18] Be as it may, if one is to judge according to his continued trajectory during the first years of the twenty-first century, Elejalde is still trying to challenge himself while continuing his involvement in that cinema of excess or "cine gamberro," as may be seen in his participation in Javier Rebollo's *Marujas asesinas* (*Lady Killers,* 2001) and *Locos por el sexo* (*Crazy for Sex,* 2006), or in his own *Torapia* (2004) and *Año Mariano* (*Mary's Year,* 2000). Moreover, as if to confirm his "othering" non-conformist commitment and his continued peripheral dialogue, he has stepped up his collaboration with young or new directors, such as his work with Ray Loriga in *La pistola de mi hermano* (*My Brother's Gun,* 1997) and with two Catalan newcomers, Jaume Balagueró's *Los sin nombre* (*The Nameless,* 1999) and Joaquim Oristrell's *Novios* (*Boyfriends,* 1999). It is also worth remembering here his contribution to *El calentito* (*The Calentito Bar,* 2005), the film directed by Chus Gutiérrez, one of the most promising of Spain's new women directors whose *Poniente (Dusk,* 2006) and *Retorno a Hansala*(*Return to Hansala,* 2008) have established her prominent role in the depiction of Spain's most pressing historical Other, the racially marked immigrant from Africa. Ultimately, therefore, Karra Elejalde has remained true to his rebellious origins and to his uncanny assumption of cinematic stardom. An uncanny status that continues to mark him as the bearer of the Basque margins within the Spanish imaginary. Such a paradoxical position may be emblematized in his last performance as the volatile, self-effacing actor who tries to embody the figure of a cinematically recreated Christopher Columbus in Iciar Bollain's *También la lluvia* (*Even the Rain,* 2010). One would be hard pressed to find a better emblem of Spanish historical appropriation of an uncanny other than that of Columbus himself. Elejalde's casting as such a figure, in one of the least celebratory renditions of his story to emerge from Spain, is in itself a telling document. In the context of this paper, it may tell the story that Spain's new masculinities and some of its old historical others have finally reached the big screen.

Elorriaga, Arias, and Bisquert, or the Basque Body Politic on Display

Unlike Karra Elejalde, Patxi Bisquert and Xabier Elorriaga arrived to the cinematic screens almost by chance. In Bisquert's case, that chance was based on the fact that he had been one of the ETA members actually serving time in Segovia's jail just until a few months before the historical escape from that prison carried out by a group of ETA inmates together with the Catalan anarchist Oriol Solé Sugranyes. In fact, the political activist soon to become one of the leading actors within Basque cinema was truly surprised when he was asked to take part in Imanol Uribe's remarkable attempt at merging "cinema vérité," and action thriller in *La fuga de Segovia* (*The Segovia Breakout*, 1981), the second film in Uribe's Basque trilogy: "I never thought I would be an actor. I enjoyed show business only as a spectator, nothing else. It was the friends who were producing *La Fuga de Segovia* who got me into it. I didn't think it twice because I believed that such a story had to be known by many people.[19] The parallelism between real life and cinematic fiction was, therefore, the first and foremost reason why Patxi Bisquert was chosen to participate in Imanol Uribe's chronicle of the historical events described in the film. Thus, from the very beginning of his career, Patxi Bisquert was identified and cast as a *gudari*, both in the sense of a political fighter for the Basque cause against the oppression of Franco's dictatorship, and as the gendered male stereotype described by Rob Stone and Helen Jones. Unlike Elejalde, and partially Elorriaga, Bisquert has always been very clear regarding his political convictions:

> He tells me that he was always involved in trying to solve the social and political problems of the Basque Country, which is his own, and that he is one of the founders of *Euskadiko Eskerra*.[20]

If Patxi Bisquert's first acting part was mostly due to his own historical relationship with the events described in *La fuga de Segovia* (1981), his crucial role as the lead character in Montxo Armendáriz's *Tasio* (1984) allowed him to achieve an almost immediate iconicity, which may be explained ideologically by the fact that, as Tasio, he embodied the most idealized values of the Basque rural *baserri* world: rootedness, courage, strength, and rebellious perseverance. This allowed him to occupy the two sides of the Basque nationalist male ideal: the political *gudari* and the safe-keeper of the Basque rural world. In gendered terms, with Patxi Bisquert's arrival, Basque cinema appeared to have found its first true heteronormative male star. Despite Armendáriz's expressed desire to film "a story about a non-heroic man, someone who, without being well known, had some merit in his daily life,"[21] there are several moments in the film where Tasio's strength of character and moral fiber is magnified so that he ends up acquiring an iconic stature as an emblem of the aforementioned idealized sense of Basque masculinity. One of such moments is the heroic attempt to save his neighbor Angel's son by rescuing him from falling inside the charcoal pit. Another clear instance is seen in the sequence that follows Tasio's declaration of independence, which already presents his figure not as anonymous but as the very center of all the villagers' gazes, since he will be the most decisive *pelotari* in the Basque ball game played as part of the local festivities. The collective significance of this moment is underscored by Armendáriz's framing technique. Just as he will do during the wedding banquet scene later in the film, the director creates a sense of a natural theater, this time using a middle long shot that doubles the framing of the outdoors ball court, which is outlined first by the open rectangular line of the spectators, among which we can see some old men wearing typical Basque berets; and then is immediately framed again by the green lines of the valley and the mountains in the background. It is obvious, therefore, that Armendáriz is here following the path set by Néstor Basterretxea and Fernando Larruqert in their foundational documentary film *Ama Lur* (*Mother Earth*, 1968), especially in its idealized/ing representation of the intimate connection between nature, work, art, and sport as the most basic human activities in the Basque rural world. Tasio's figure, moreover, will be magnified not only by being cheered and later congratulated by everybody but also by the fact that he plays on bare feet. In this sense, beyond the traditional impact of the open hand against the ball, the film adds yet another layer to that mythical notion of "la piel contra la piedra" ("the skin against the stone") that was one of the central emblems in the Basque prehistoric caves, also highlighted in *Ama Lur.* This entire sequence, moreover, becomes a clear forerunner of the use of this very metaphor in Julio Medem's documentary film *La pelota vasca. La piel contra la piedra* (*Basque Ball. Skin Against Stone*, 2003). The use of the open ball court as natural theater where the fourth wall is nature itself will be underlined by its transformation into an outdoors dance floor right after the ball game is finished. In between these two collective events, however, Armendáriz will offer us a subtle and yet quite significant moment of homosocial and quasi homoerotic bonding between Tasio and his friend Luis: "Anda que te has puesto bueno con tu mania de jugar descalzo!" ("See what you've done to yourself with your crazy thing of playing barefeet!"), will be Luis's tender reproach while the camera shows his hands almost caressing Tasio's partly bloodied feet. "Y qué, no voy a espiazar un par de alpargatas en cada partido!" ("So what, I'm not going to break a pair of espadrille in every game!") (*Tasio*. Film script) will be Tasio's firm but friendly response that shows not only the kind of manliness his friend admires and feels so attached to, but also indicates the self-consciousness of his humble origins. This moment appears also as a culmination of the lifelong admiration (and attraction) felt by Luis towards Tasio, which was already inscribed in the film when Luis, as an adolescent, congratulated Tasio for his courageous "rite of passage," after he dared to tend to the "carbonera" (charcoal pit) on his own and received a pair of long trousers from his father as token of his newly gained adulthood.

Bisquert's composite figure of a historical fighter and a fictional performer will accompany him throughout his career and it may explain why his embodiment of Armendáriz's cinematic take on Anastasio Ochoa, the real life "carbonero" he had met and got to admire while filming his documentary film *Carboneros de Navarra*, was destined to become not only one of the most enduring emblems of Basque masculinity, but also one of the central icons of an idealized representation of the Basque (nationalist) rural self.[22] From this perspective, the homosocial, if not homoerotic, component just described becomes especially relevant in its inscription of a frequently hidden layer in the subject formation and representation of the (Basque) nationalist normative heterosexual male.

That crossing between reality and fiction, moreover, was to mark Bisquert's own narrative casting throughout the eighties within Basque cinema. If we obviate for a moment his earlier roles in Pedro Olea's *Akelarre* (1983) and in Alfonso Ungría's *La conquista de Albania* (*The Conquest of Albania*, 1983), Patxi Bisquert was mostly to be cast either as a political fighter or as a rebellious strong character who always survived his predicament. This is the case, for instance, in Alfonso Ungría's short film *Ehun Metro* (*A Hundred Meters*, 1985), which was an adaptation of Ramon Saizarbitoria's novel of the same title. This film presented the final moments of an ETA fighter, Jon, who was being chased by the police in the old quarters of *Donosti*.   Bisquert's performance enhanced the end-of the-road anxiety of somebody facing death while the film's counterpointed structure and the use of the flashbacks allowed Ungría to make an ironic statement regarding the two *Donostias* of the time, that is, the persistence of the "esplendoroso marco/ beautiful setting" image over that of a city torn by real problems.[23]

The two sides of Patxi Bisquert's cinematic persona, that of the (ex)-ETA activist and that of the heroic survivor, found artistic expression in the next two Basque films that cast him as Amiel, the lead role as the falsely accused *arrantzale (fisherman)* in Anjel Lertxundi's *Kareletik* (*Overboard*, 1987), and as Peio, the co-protagonist who is an ex-ETA member returning home after having left the armed struggle, in Ernesto del Río's *El amor de ahora* (*Loving Today,* 1987). The casting of Patxi Bisquert as Peio is certainly one of the clearest examples of using the actor as a signifier, given the symbolic resonance of Bisquert's cinematic persona after his performance as Tasio. In del Río's film, Peio returns home to get reunited with his father, who is waiting for him in his *baserri* as if time had not eloped and as if the political turmoil was something that belonged elsewhere. And yet, as the painful process of reinserttion between Peio and his wife Arantza, who is also an ex-ETA fighter, clearly shows, there will be no place in the film where one can escape from the shadows of the past as they continue to project their spectral gaze on the present. Ultimately, Bisquert's own appearance becomes the marker of that impossible return home, the impossibility, that is, of absorbing and healing the deep split between the rural and the urban worlds that has been at the heart of the endemic violence in *Euskadi*.   Thus, in choosing Bisquert, del Río has an easier job of emphasizing that invisible yet highly present cultural split that the film so efficiently chronicles.

Bisquert's cinematic *gudari* persona had already become almost established after his roles as the young lover Unai Esparza in Pedro Olea's *Akelarre* (1983) and as the faithful companion to Luis de Beaumont, the visionary prince who led the expedition of Navarrese warriors against those faraway ghostly enemies, the role played by Xabier Elorriaga, in Alfonso Ungría's *La conquista de Albania* (1983). There is, however, a peculiar moment in Ungría's film that becomes an uncanny anticipation of Bisquert's role as Tasio. I am referring to the early stages in the preparation of the expedition to conquer Albania when both the commoners and the council of noblemen are debating the advantages and problems of such an undertaking.

It will be in this context that the would-be expeditionary played by Bisquert utters the following statement: "Cazar bandidos, no es lo mismo que hacer la guerra." ("To hunt for bandits is not the same as to fight a war." Film script). Indeed, as the film will show, the metaphor of hunting becomes especially adept in describing a war that is presented almost as an impossible hunt, or to play a bit with the contiguity of the two words in English, as a phantasmatic war that haunts the characters from beginning to end. Like Unai Esparza, the relentless lover of Garazi de Ochoa, Patxi Bisquert's character in Pedro Olea's historical tale *Akelarre* (1983) suffers a bit from the film's general lack of mystery or ambiguity and the figure of Unai ends up becoming a kind of clichéd version of the ill-starred lovers of all time. What the film truly achieves, on the other hand, is to produce a powerful allegorical rendition of the Spanish will to conquer and reduce any attempt at "otherness," be it cultural, sexual, or religious. And, in this sense, the performances by Patxi Bisquert and Sílvia Munt and their sexual celebration of freedom as part of those "lugareños de vida distinta" becomes truly convincing, besides offering one of the clearest instances of historical parallelism between the world portrayed in the film and the repression of Basque cultural and political difference suffered under the Franco regime and its own witch hunting. And, by the implications of Sílvia Munt's own narrative casting, it also extends that allegorical reading to the repression suffered by Catalonia, the second irreducible "other" within the Spanish State. In keeping with that "cine periférico" notion alluded to by Imanol Uribe that I mentioned earlier, Patxi Bisquert, just like Xabier Elorriaga had done, also found an artistic home in Catalan screens, thus reinforcing that symbolic blurring of the Spanish "other" in cinematic terms. Bisquert's migration, unlike Elorriaga's, though, was mainly due to the financial crisis lived in Basque cinema after the commercial failures of big budget films that had been partly produced with public moneys offered by the Basque autonomous government. Indeed, after a brief excursion in the role of Pedrarías in Carlos Saura's *El Dorado* (1988), Bisquert was cast in seven Catalan films: Francesc Bellmunt's *Un negre amb un saxo* (*A Black Man with a Saxophone*, 1989), Ferran Llagostera's *El gran sol* (*The Big Sun*, 1989) and *Terranova* (1991), Jordi Grau's *La punyalada* (*The Stabbing*, 1990), Andreu Martín's *Sauna* (1990), and *La Teranyina* (The *Cobweb*, 1990) and *Havanera 1820* (1992), both directed by Toni Verdaguer. In between, and up to today, he has reappeared in several more or less secondary roles in Basque films, such as that of the press owner Julen in Antxon Eceiza's *Ke arteko egunak* (*Days of Smoke,* 1990), or as Luis, another ill-starred lover in Koldo Izagirre's *Amor en off* (1992), as Satur in Ernesto Tellería's *Suerte* (*Luck*, 1997). He was also cast as one of the *maquis* in Montxo Armendáriz's *Silencio roto* (*Broken Silence*, 2001), and as José Luis in Koldo Serra's *Bosque de sombras* (*Back Woods*, 2006). Very much unlike the final familiar appropriation of Xabier Elorriaga's Basque otherness by Spanish audiences, however, the resilience of Patxi Bisquert's narrative casting or the iconic and "uncanny," in Joseba Gabilondo's sense of the term, quality of his Basque othering presence may be illustrated in one of his latest roles, when he plays the toughest of the ETA members used as hostages in Daniel Monzón's big box office hit *Celda 211* (*Cell 211*, 2009).

Unlike Patxi Bisquert, Xabier Elorriaga was not imprisoned but had to flee *Euskadi* due to his political activities. And then, after more than fifteen years living in Catalonia, where he had gone to try his hand in theater in the famous *Adrià Gual* company directed by Ricard Salvat, he ended up graduating in Journalism and teaching "TV genres" at the *Universitat Autònoma de Barcelona*. It was in Catalonia, and again almost by chance, that he was offered a minor role that ended up becoming the leading one in Antoni Ribas' historical docudrama *La ciutat cremada* (*The Burned City*, 1976). Elorriaga's long stay in Catalonia, together with his Latin American origin at the heart of the Basque diaspora, first in Venezuela and later in Chile, also turns him into an "other" to most actors with no migrant or hybrid biographical elements. And yet again, it will be this "other" and different persona that allows him to attain a cinematic centrality, first in Catalonia, later in the Basque Country and, finally, in Spain as a whole. If Imanol Uribe had been the first son of the Basque diaspora to achieve a prominent role in the context of the emergent Basque cinema, Xabier Elorriaga was to become the first face of the Basque exile to make it into a leading iconic position, thus reinforcing the uncanny nature of a possible Basque star system. Xabier Elorriaga's Basque origins, however, were neither weakened nor forgotten during his youth years, as had been the case in so many Basque families in the diaspora, according to Gloria Totoricagüena:

> *Euskera* as a factor of individual Basque ethnic identity has lost much of its importance among these diaspora populations. In *Euskal Herria* itself, various areas were totally hispanicized by the mid-1800s, and later, during the Franco era, Basque was outlawed as a means of communication. Consequently, many emigrants of the political-exile era did not themselves speak Basque. Though

Basques are extremely proud of their unique language and its complexity, most do not consider it an important factor in their own personal ethnicity…Overall, only 5 percent use Basque regularly, and another five percent use Basque every day, switching back and forth between languages and using Basque equally with other languages.[24]

Elorriaga's family not only formed part of that five percent, but, as the actor himself recalls, his use of the Basque language was under strict maternal surveillance:

My family was politically committed, especially my mother. I still speak *Euskara* and I think about the most important things in that language. When I came back to Spain, my mother used to return my letters when a single word in Spanish had found its place on the page.[25]

It seems perfectly fitting, therefore, that Imanol Uribe chose such an obedient son to play the role of another very prominent obedient son, that of Iñaki, Mikel's older brother in *La muerte de Mikel* (*Mikel's Death*, 1984), Uribe's successful familiar allegory, which was the last film in hi so-called Basque trilogy. If Mikel (Imanol Arias) portrayed the rebellion, both sexual and political, against the status quo embodied in that stern matriarchal figure —arguably the most impressive phallic mother in the whole of Basque cinema who, interestingly enough, was remarkably portrayed by Catalan actress Montserrat Salvador—, Xabier Elorriaga's Iñaki becomes the perfect replica as the uptight, reasonable, and sometimes slightly patronizing older brother who always remains *au dessus de la melée*, side by side with his mother, thus offering not only one of Elorriaga's most convincing portrayals but one of the most powerful gendered representations of Euskadi´s body politic as a patriarchal matriarchy. There is a double coincidence worth mentioning here since it speaks directly about the uncanny nature of most Basque cinematic icons. I am thinking of the fact that Xabier Elorriaga changed the order of his surnames to adopt his maternal one as his most cherished identity marker and to the fact that his first cinematic role, as mentioned earlier, was that of the petit bourgeois son of a Catalan family whose matriarch was also played by Montserrat Salvador in Antoni Ribas' *La ciutat cremada* (1976). Such an uncanny coincidence may also be explained by the narrative casting that constantly criss-crossed the Catalan/Basque screen barrier, as may be clearly illustrated in the case of Sílvia Munt, whose acting persona was fixated by her extraordinary embodiment of Natàlia/Colometa, the allegorical mother that stood for Catalonia's struggle in Francesc Betriu's *La plaça del Diamant* (*Diamond's*

Square, 1982), the historical cinematic adaptation of Mercè Rodoreda's famous novel of the same title. Indeed, there seems to be little doubt that the series of tragic and/or heroic (m)otherly figures played by Sílvia Munt in Pedro Olea's *Akelarre* (1983), Juanma Bajo Ulloa's *Alas de mariposa* (*Butterfly Wings*, 1991), or Montxo Armendáriz's *Secretos del corazón* (*Secrets of the Heart*, 1997) obey this rule of the narrative casting. In this sense, Montserrat Salvador's unforgettable performance as the terrible mother in *La muerte de Mikel* becomes one of the earliest and most extraordinary examples of a narrative casting that contributes to creating a truly uncanny Basque star system. It is within this constant criss-crossing of narrative castings between *Euskadi* and Catalonia that Xabier Elorrioaga finds a privileged position, besides being, as I have already pointed out, the clearest instance of a migrant subject, both biographically and in acting terms, an emblematic (and enigmatic) migrant subject position that will become his most distinctive characteristic. Ultimately, however, this uncanny othering face of the Basque exile will be appropriated by most Spaniards. Indeed, after his successful embodiment of the character of Enrique in Ana Diosdado's "Anillos de Oro" (*Golden Rings*), Elorriaga's became a constant face in other Spanish television series, some of which enjoyed wide audiences like "Hospital Central (*Central Hospital*, 2001) and "El Comisario" (The *Police Inspector*, 2006). His long cherished ideal of spectatorial identification was finally achieved at the expense of, or perhaps as the culmination of, his Basque othering persona. Elorriaga's gesture will be replicated in a much larger scale by another Basque (inner) exile. I am referring to Imanol Arias, whom very few Spaniards remember today in his groundbreaking role as Mikel, the homosexual political activist in Uribe's *La muerte de Mikel* but recognize in the streets as the charismatic Antonio Alcántara, the endearing *pater familias* in the nostalgic and enormously successful Spanish television series "Cuéntame como pasó!" It seems quite fitting, therefore, that Chris Perriam chose him as the first "Spanish star" in his already mentioned study. Interestingly enough, as Perriam notes, from the beginning of his career, Imanol Arias was able to occupy both positions almost at the same time. He was soon considered "Spain's Sweetheart" while also becoming the most exemplary in "representing crisis at the intersection of gender, power, desire, and social process."[26] Nowhere is this most evident than in his role as Mikel, as Perriam himself observes:

> In Uribe's *La muerte de Mikel,* this is acutely apparent. The film makes Arias a
> point of intersection of sexual and national(ist) politics as well as being of interest
> for its part in an Oedipal drama with allegorical resonances in national and state
> politics.[27]

Elsewhere,[28] I have analyzed in some detail the significance of Uribe's film, both by itself and also by its contribution to the entire Basque trilogy that, more or less consciously, embodied cinematically his own personal process of a migrant subject returning home to Euskadi, a process that, as seen first in *La muerte de Mikel* and later in *Dias contados* (*Counted Days*, 1994), moved from fascination to horror. Here, I would like to briefly revisit the issues surrounding what we might call "spectral masculinities" that take central stage in Uribe's film and mark an imaginary turning point in Euskadi's self-representation. For, as Andrew Parker, Mary Russo, Doris Sommer and Patricia Yaeger, the four editors of *Nationalisms and Sexualities*, rightly remind us:

> Though undeveloped in his analysis, Anderson's comparison enables the crucial
> recognition that –like gender– nationality is a relational term whose identity derives
> from its inherence in a system of differences…But the very fact that such identities
> depend constitutively on differences means that nations are forever haunted by their
> various definitional others. Hence, on the one hand, the nation's insatiable need to
> administer difference through violent acts of segregation, censorship, economic
> coercion, physical torture, police brutality. And hence, on the other, the nation's
> insatiable need for representational labor to supplement its founding ambivalence,
> the lack of self-presence at its origin or in its essence.[29]

Both "national needs" are clearly inscribed in Uribe's *La muerte de Mikel,* where inner segregation, state brutality, and ghostly enemies are all conjured up in one of the most powerful critical renditions of the heterosexual normative representation of the nation in the entire Basque and Spanish cinematic canons. In fact, the entire film is structured around the haunting presence of the other's death. Mikel's dead body is doubly allegorical, both as a replica of the Christian ritual as the sacrificial victim, the scapegoat that binds the community together or, at least, allows its symbolic order to remain intact; and also as the marker of the totemic logic of the fratricidal struggle over the house of the father. As in many of the most significant Basque movies —Arantxa Lazkano's *Urte Ilunak* (*The Dark Years*, 1992), Juanma Bajo Ulloa's *Alas de mariposa* (*Butterfly Wings*, 1991) or Daniel Calparsoro's *Salto al vacío* (*Leap into the Void*, 1993)—, the father always occupies a ghostly position as completely absent or as a castrated absent/present figuration. Uribe's personal version of this symbolic structure will substitute the prescriptive Oedipal parricide with a remarkable performance of the "specter of fratricide" that, in historical terms, anticipates the political reality of an autonomous Basque Country whose own police are put in charge of that "national need" of repressing serious political or sexual deviances. The "ghostly enemy" becomes then interiorized, as Begoña Aretxaga explains:

> Because the violence ocurring between Basque police and radical-nationalist activists falls within the "imagined community" of the Basque nation (in contrast to a former symbolic structure in which the "Basque people" was opposed to the "Spanish state"), such violence has evoked for many Basques the specter of fratricide and a corresponding deep anxiety over national (Basque) identity.[30]

It is, indeed, this "specter of fratricide" that becomes the narrative center in *Mikel's Death.* Thus, the basic split in Basque politics between the PNB (Nationalist Basque Party) and *Herri Batasuna* is directly inscribed in the rivalry between the two brothers, Iñaki (Xabier Elorriaga) and Mikel (Imanol Arias), who live by the shadow of the overpowering matriarch in the (Oedipal) family metaphor that structures Uribe's *Mikel's Death.* This Cainite motif will be further explored by Ana Díez's *Ander eta Yul* (*Andrew and Yul*, 1988) by having the two friends of the film's title be "religious brothers" since they were best pals in the Divinity School of their youth. In this way, Díez's film conflates the family metaphor with the sacramental/excremental level of the "specter of fratricide" mentioned by Aretxaga. In the context of this study, moreover, it resonates in anticipation of Roberto Castón's film *Ander*, by giving that same name, the classical synonym for maleness, to the lead character who will fall quite short from the *gudari* identity rather masochistically occupied by his "brother" Yul. *Mikel's Death* and, to a lesser extent, *Ander eta Yul* are, moreover, the first Basque films to represent homosexuality as the social difference that triggers the violence of the intolerant forces in *Euskadi.* And, as it will be the case in Ana Díez's film, one part of those intolerant forces will be Mikel´s own *gudari* brothers, a predicament clearly summarized by Rob Stone and Helen Jones:

> Displacement is illustrated by Uribe's *La muerte de Mikel* (*Mikel's Death*, 1983) in which a radical Basque nationalist's coming out as gay prompts his political comrades to reject him. Even on a visual level, Mikel's status as *gudari* is undermined by his physical, and therefore symbolic marginalization from his peers: at party headquarters, for example, Mikel is the only man without a beard. Mikel may lead the street protest wrapped in the Basque flag and triumph in Basque sports that are traditional displays of supposedly heterosexual masculinity and virility, but

his private actions see him retreat from the stereotype to his truer homosexual Self. When his sexuality becomes public, Mikel's colleagues withdraw his candidature from the local elections and he is erased from public view because this space does not permit plural versions of Basqueness, nor any challenge to the rigidity of the gender stereotyping on which it is based.[31]

The other intolerant forces in front of Mikel's homosexuality are also represented in familiar terms, both in the sense of invoking the Oedipal phallic mother and also as indicator of Uribe's own misogynistic position by recurring once more to the mother-monster figuration that has appeared as a true gender limitation in so many of the most interesting Basque films of the nineties.[32] Despite its arguable ideological consistence, the portrayal of Doña María Luisa, Iñaki's and Mikel's "phantasmatic Mother," becomes the true cinematic landmark of the film, as Santos Zunzunegui has rightly observed:

What happens is that the true frame of the story —the one that *de facto* confers sense to the events narrated — is placed elsewhere. I am referring, first, to that enigmatic shot placed very early in the film in which, after the first hints of the frictions between Begoña and Mikel, the latter is seen, in an ostentatious high angle shot, staring from the balcony towards an unidentified woman all clad in black advancing by the dock only to stop and look up towards the young pharmacist house, all of this while a zoom isolates her from the context. This shot, placed as it is just before the couple's visit to the mother's house, does not find an easy justification. In fact, it finds its true meaning when it is related to the final shot of the film where "la madre de Mikel" (could it be an alternative title for the film?) is shot in a low angle travelling [at a similar balcony] staring out and lost in deep thoughts. If I have described those shots in detail is to clearly establish that to the story of intolerance and political manipulation, which is obviously set in motion from the beginning, one finds the superimposition of another story, of clear melodramatic overtones, that places Mikel's personal itinerary between two poles inscribing the acceptance of his homosexuality (and the love he feels for Fama) and the rupture that such an acceptance effects on his domineering and socially enslaved to convention mother.[33]

Ultimately, as suggested above, the film may be seen also as Imanol Uribe's vital mirror stage, in the sense that it reflects his own predicament or the impossible belonging in that Basque home he had dreamed of. Mikel's "non serviam" is, in a way, a narrative transposition of Uribe's own rejection of a world that had fascinated him at first:

When Mikel abandons the party headquarters with his "sois unos curas de mierda" (You're a bunch of shitty priests!), it is Uribe himself who is showing all his disenchantment in front of a world that had at first fascinated him and that has ended by completely disappointing him.[34]

Carlos Roldán's words are quite accurate in their characterization of Uribe's film as a document of the political "desencanto" (disenchanment) that was the most frequent response to the ideological and historical process of the Spanish transition to democracy and its pact of silence. What Roldán's account does not reveal, however, is that Uribe's initial attraction to and fascination with *Euskadi* was already inscribed in a peculiar national fantasy, a sort of Lacanian self-discovery. In other words, when Uribe recognizes himself in the mirror of the Basque Country, he sees himself at the same time as subject and as object, as an active participant and as a passive, almost voyeuristic, spectator. Or, to put it differently, as a migrant subject. That position was partly due to his having been born, like Xabi Elorriaga, in the Basque diaspora; but it also responded to a certain self-imposed distance, a distance that allowed him to occupy an insider/outsider role which was, ultimately, what gave him access to Euskadi's politics and its cinematic representation. In the context of *La muerte de Mikel*, moreover, such a position was the one given to Martín, the exiled Chilean doctor who appears as the most ambivalent figure in the entire film and who, despite having betrayed Mikel in his police confession, ultimately holds the key to his enigmatic death because of his being in charge of Mikel's body autopsy. The figure of Martín (of Uribe?) appears as doubly other, as a variation of the "foreigner" intruding in the intimacies of the Basque nation, or, as a variation of the inner ghostly enemy, the "brotherly friend" turned "spectral enemy." This predicament may explain the apparent paradox that the most emblematic director of the new Basque cinema may have been an outsider, even a voyeur, whose "innocent" gaze always aimed at unmasking the mystery surrounding the violence of the Basque body politic.

Ander/Aita: Spectral Refigurations of the House of the Father in Basque Cinema

> En la mitología vasca, la casa o *etxe* es un recinto sagrado y un centro de convergencia entre los vivos y los muertos en plano de igualdad. [In Basque mithology, the house or *etxe* is a sacred space and a center of convergence between the living and the dead on equal footing.][35]

At the very heart of the two films that I have chosen to conclude this essay, there is the essential presence of the Basque house, be it the rural *baserri* (farmstead) of Ander's family in Kortezubi or the noble mansion of the Murguia family in Astigarraga, the small Guipuzcoan village where José

María de Orbe was born. This fundamental coincidence would not be too meaningful unless considered in the context of a gendered analysis of the cinematic figurations of the Basque Country and its othering masculinities. Indeed, as suggested earlier, both films can be seen as radical subversions of the traditional family metaphor which had always been constructed within the parameters of the Oedipal narrative. Or, to put it in geopolitical terms, both films inscribe themselves as markers of a trans/postnational space wherein the Spanish/Basque Oedipal struggle is bypassed from within and without. In *Ander* (*Andrew*, 2009), for instance, we are presented with the literal reality of the continuation of the Basque traditional model of rural life thanks to the acceptance of an alternative family formed by two homosexual men, Ander, the son and inheritor of the *baserri*, José, the Peruvian immigrant whose hired labor has proved essential, and Reme, the motherly prostitute who has also had to break loose from her own traditional family romance. In *Aita* (*Father*, 2010), it will be the care of an old housekeeper and his friend, the local priest, who will preserve literally alive the ghostly presence of the familiar past in the Murguia mansion owned by the director himself. Interestingly enough, both films, despite their transgressive nature (or maybe because of it), are in keeping with those "peripheral practices" that I outlined earlier. Thus, as I indicated earlier, Roberto Castón, the director of *Ander* is a Galician born who formed himself cinematically in Catalonia and is now the director of *Zinegoak*, the International Gay, Lesbian and Transsexual Cinema Festival in Bilbao, where the film premiered in 2009 under the auspices of the Basque Autonomous Government.[36] José María de Orbe, on the other hand, is a Basque born who studied direction in the American Film Institute in Los Angeles and who has created most of his work on publicity and film in Barcelona. In fact, *Aita* is produced by Luis Miñarro, one of the most important Catalan producers of new and experimental film in Spain and elsewhere. Another fundamental commonality of the two films discussed here is their culmination of one of the most recurrent elements in Basque cinema: the absent/present father figure, or, as mentioned in the title of this section, their spectral refiguration of the house of the father. Thus, right after the funeral of his mother, and after the first truly panoramic view of the valley and the mountains facing Ander's *baserri,* we will hear him utter this question: "¿Soy tu hijo?" ("Am I your son?") Evaristo's astonished and heartfelt reply cannot hide the fact that he has been Ander's mother's true love and, such reality, in this moment of final confessions and realizations, is more important than any legal fantasy of paternity. With that panoramic view from the balcony of Ander's *baserri*, moreover, the director is underlining the true opening up of a closed symbolic economy, the totemic logic of debt and sacrifice always already inscribed in the paternal law of heterosexual normative filiation. With Ander's acceptance of the other parental figure and of his own homosexual identity, the ghostly absent presence of his dead father no longer obtains. In the case of José María de Orbe´s film, *Aita*, this historical exorcism is carried out metafictitiously, the chosen vehicle being the history of Basque cinema itself:

> Just like the archeologist of the film's prologue that excavates the bones buried under the house foundations, I rescued fragments of the oldest Basque cinema so that I could remain faithful to real images that were spatially and temporally related to the history of the house...The present of the house remains thus associated in the fiction with cinema's destiny. A cinema that is a noble art that observes its own decadence and fights to survive with terror and fascination.[37]

In Orbe´s film, the house of his historical and biological father coalesces phantasmatically with the house of (Basque) cinema. Thus, his exorcism conjures up one of the central tenets of that cinema: its (in)visibility.[38] Or, to follow Orbe's suggestion, its ghostly (or uncanny) existence. In "Misterios de la materia viva," Carlos F. Heredero provides a suggestive reading of that predicament:

> Because *Aita* and its corollary (*Aita. Carta al hijo/ Father. Letter to the Son*) gravitate around the notion of emptiness...And it is precisely that emptiness – dramatical, narrative, architectonic, but also sculptural: Oteiza vibrates under its folds– that ends up filling those images that take over the place of the house, that absorb it completely, and that achieve a full screen ultimate decomposition of the cinematic material and, with it, a dissolution of any possible history.[39]

There are at least four ways to interpret the lack or emptiness that Heredero reads as essential to an understanding of Orbe's film. I have already indicated the first one —namely, the historical and existential emptiness inscribed in the Basque body politic by means of that constant recurrence of the ghostly absent/present father figure, which, to name only a few basic films, reappears in Imanol Uribe's *La muerte de Mikel* (1984), Juanma Bajo Ulloa's *Alas de mariposa* (*Butterfly Wings*, 1991), Arantxa Lazcano's *Urte Illunak* (*The Dark Years*, 1992), or in Daniel Calparsoro's *Salto al vacío* (*Leap into the Void*, 1993). The second aspect suggested deals with the very notion of any subjective sense of identity and its relationship with lack, as

Kaja Silverman reminds us: "The implicit starting point for virtually every formulation this book will propose is the assumption that lack of being is the irreducible condition of subjectivity."[40] A third reading entails what we might call, following the lead of many of his practitioners, the "zero existence" of Basque cinema as an autonomous historical entity. This non-existence of the house of the father in terms of Basque cinema might explain the historical exile of many Basque directors who had to find a different home in other imaginary houses or narratives, often ending up engrossing the master narrative of an all-encompassing Spanish cinema. The clearest and most illustrious example of such a gesture is represented by the figure of Víctor Erice, who, as Carlos F. Heredero also acknowledges in the case of Orbe's film, occupies that paternal position. Erice's case is particularly significant since he achieves a kind of double phantasmatic identity, as both the (in)visible father of the new Spanish and the new Basque cinema. Finally, as also suggested in Heredero's quote, there is another spectral aesthetic paternity clearly invoked in Orbe's film, the one occupied by the figure of Jorge Oteiza and his theory of the "cromlech," or the empty artifact that holds the essence of the human artistic endeavor.[41] The phantasmatic white light that haunts the housekeeper throughout the film and that the director inscribes in the open moonlight circle of one of the house windows as an empty hole into the skies is but Orbe's most markedly Oteizan metaphor. A metaphor, on the other hand, that seems to replicate in reverse that of the dark pit in the forest which Julio Medem also emphasized as the central metaphor in his remarkable first feature film *Vacas* (*Cows*, 1992), thus reinforcing the notion that Orbe's film reinscribes the history of Basque cinema, not merely with images from its historical beginnings, such as the ones belonging to *Edurne, modista bilbaína* (*Edurne, the Seamstress from Bilbao*), commonly considered to be the oldest Basque feature film, but also with echoes of contemporary Basque films. Interestingly enough, it will be this phantastmatic inscription of the Oteizan "aesthetic void" that seems to have become the most noted in the local reception of Orbe's film, as these words by Mikel G. Gurpegui in "Casa tomada" illustrate:

> La casa. La casa del padre. La casa en la que dormitan siglos de historia. La casa degradada, invadida por la hiedra, la maleza o las goteras. La casa con huesos que desenterrar. La casa vasca y vacía, o sea, de Oteiza. [The house. The father's house. The house where centuries of history sleep. The decayed house, taken over by ivy, weeds, and leaks. The house full of bones to dig up. The Basque empty house, that is, the Oteizan house.][42]

Does that Oteizan filiation as the common point in the (Basque) critical reception of the film turn José María de Orbe's *Aita* into an essentialist cinematic refiguration of the house of the father as basic metaphor for Euskadi itself? The question keeps reappearing in many of the interviews with the director whose answers seem to feed such a possible reductive reading. Thus, when asked about the trans/postnational identity of his film by Urkiri Salaberria, "Is *Aita* Basque, Catalan, Spanish or European cinema? Or is it simply Orbe''s cinema?," Orbe's answer was:

> *Aita* is Basque, Catalan and Spanish cinema. Above all, it is Basque cinema, not only because it has been shot in the Basque Country, but because it strives to find some Basque essence (cierta esencia de lo vasco).[43]

And when Pere Vall asked him again about the symbolic significance of that house, "Y la casa... ¿es un símbolo del País Vasco? ("And the house, is it a symbol of the Basque Country?"), Orbe's answer is again somewhat mystifying:

> No, the Basque Country is more complex and rich, although it is true that in this old house the most quotidian and the most extraordinary coexist just like in our country. In any event, the work I have done is too intimate as to represent something so large and that is not in decadence. This house is an injury effected by time. We all pass through it, and it remains there.[44]

Orbe's peculiar word choice, especially that allusion to the house as an "injury," highly recalls the use of the same metaphor to illustrate another of the recurrent elements in any attempt to describe Euskadi's current and past history: its foundational injury or split, both its geopolitical split between sovereign nation-states, such as France and Spain, and its inner split in its body politic.[45] My own description of the Basque cultural imaginary as a whole sounds, in retrospect, like an echo of the symbolic import of Orbe's film.[46]

Despite their radically different registers and ambitions, both José María de Orbe's *Aita* and Roberto Castón's *Ander* also have in common another crucial aspect: their minimalism. Indeed, both films structure themselves following a strict cinematic economy that relies heavily on symmetry and repetition and that formally reinscribes the most significant of polarities in social terms: the public/private divide. In *Ander*, the central space will be the kitchen table, which we will see once and again in symmetrical shots from the viewpoint of an invisible television set, which will also be the recurrent position of the camera. Thus, we will watch Ander's family as they are watching us, as they are returning our gaze as spectators/intruders. In fact, the position of intruder or newcomer in that domestic space will always be marked by the closest proximity to that invisible television set. In front, at the head of the table, there will always be Ander himself, to the right, his mother, and to the left, his sister, both named Arantxa, as if to reinforce that nuclear symmetry. When José, the Peruvian hired hand, sits down unawares in Ander's chair, the mother's horrified look prompts an immediate explanation by her daughter, Arantxa: "That was my father's place and now it is Ander's." The day Evaristo is finally invited to have dinner with the family, he will also sit at that corner of the table closest to the television set. This time Ander will use the television as a true barrier since he asks Evaristo to hand him the remote control only to avoid allowing him a real place and a real chance to share in the family's most intimate setting. Contrary to that moment, although obeying to the same strict visual economy, we will see how Ander later invites José to sit down by his side, in the now empty space left by Arantxa's trip to town and, thus, facing the other Arantxa, the stern matriarch who stubbornly clings to the traditional and Oedipal familiar structure, and openly rejects the intrusion of the foreigner. In using such symmetrical repetitions, moreover, Castón is clearly reinserting the public/private divide at the very heart of the house. The mother's resistance to admit "as part of the family" that temporal and foreign worker will, in fact, culminate with her initial rejection to have him share in yet another more significant table. This time, in another paradoxical symmetry, it will be Arantxa's wedding banquet table, which, as it is customary in the Basque rural world, is placed outside of the house. Castón will emphasize that *baserri* tradition in one of the film's few direct cinematic intertexts, in this case with an almost identical *mise-en-scene* as that presented by Montxo Armendáriz in his foundational Basque film *Tasio*. The frontal medium close-up shot of the long table covered by white linen and surrounded by awkwardly elegantly clad *baserritarras* is almost a replica of the same one presented by Amerndáriz in Tasio's own wedding banquet. Castón's quotation obviously reinforces the imaginary belonging of his film in that traditional and patriarchal narrative. And yet, as soon as the camera cuts to a more intimate close-up shot, we do not see the bride Arantxa or the groom Iñaki, but the figures of Ander and José, who is sitting by his side. After all, he convinced his mother that José had to be there to help him move around given his broken leg, a fact, moreover, that was the very reason why José was hired in the first place. Ander's broken leg, therefore, becomes both a marker of his symbolic castration and the perfect narrative excuse to achieve a physical proximity with José. Such a proximity will culminate, precisely, when they both leave the public wedding banquet to go to the private bathroom inside the house where that physical closeness slowly but surely evolves into an erotic encounter, which, as British critic Joseph Ewens puts it, becomes the film's "pivotal scene:"

> José's arrival is the catalyst for real narrative progression, which extends so well from the measured –not languid– opening third. His sharp Hispanic jaw-line and shirt-off manual labour awakens a latent homosexuality in Ander. Still hobbling around on crutches, he begins to follow José as he moves around the farm. This is ostensibly to ensure his work is up to scratch and to relieve the boredom of a broken leg but as the pair spend more and more time together, a burgeoning friendship quickly begins to morph into something deeper and more dangerous…All that repressed energy our lead has held back is suddenly unleashed. *Ander* could never be accused of moving at speed, but the emotional ups and downs start to flow beautifully from one *pivotal scene*. The film even manages to move seamlessly into a heart-rending sub-plot and back, without becoming emotionally overbearing or disjointed.[47]

Indeed, from that "pivotal scene," Castón's film will steadily move into developing another symmetrical story that entails the fleshing out of the mother-prostitute character, Reme, whose presence, besides that "heart-rending subplot" to which Ewens alludes, allows Castón to introduce his second basic transgression of the "narrative formation of the nation." As the editors of *Nationalisms and Sexualities* remind us:

> The idealization of motherhood by the virile fraternity would seem to entail the exclusion of all nonreproductively-oriented sexualities from the discourse of the nation.[48]

Interestingly enough, Reme's position as both mother and prostitute assures her to belong in those traditional national discourses. And yet, as it will soon be evident, Castón's special treatment of this (m)otherly figure sets him completely aside from the misogynysm of Imanol Uribe's portrayal in *La muerte de Mikel* and in that of many male Basque filmmakers to come, as I mentioned earlier in this essay. On the contrary, if anything, what the presence of Reme does in Castón's film is to introduce the reality of the female prostituted body as a space that resists national appropriations.[49] Such a symbolic position is first introduced in almost trivial geopolitical terms when Peio, the ur-male who sexually exploits and brutalizes her, is referring to her as "la murciana." Ander will soon retort: "Ella vivió en Murcia pero no es murciana, es gallega" ("She lived in Murcia but she's not from Murcia, she is from Galicia." *Ander*. Film Script). Later, in one of the first intimate sequences between Reme and José, the two outsiders-insiders of the film, Castón will let the viewers witness Reme's confession-like tale of origins:

> "¿Where are you from, José?" "From a little village near Cuzco"..."I am from Cariño. It is a village in Coruña. Do you know where Coruña is?"..."I've lived in Madrid, Salou, and Cartagena but this is different to anything else. I'm sure that it's different from Cuzco." "And why are you here?" "I'm waiting for my husband." "Is he on a trip? "He's lost. When he finds himself, he'll come back." ... "We met there, in Cartagena, almost secretly. When he finished his military service we came back to Oro. He only had that, an old house in his village in Euskadi. He had barely any family, only that."... "I had done it before but never in my husband's house. Wherever, but not there. At least when he comes back he'll find his house clean."[50]

Few people other than Basques or Galicians know that Cariño (Endearment) is truly the name of a fishing village in the coast of the A Coruña province and that Oro (Gold) is also a name of a small Guipuzcoan village. Castón's toponymic choice cannot be more appropriate in mapping out the double geopolitical symbolism of the film. In terms of any "peripheral practice" in the Spanish context, Galicia has always occupied a marginal position. And yet, due to the massive Galician migration to Latin America, most Spaniards were identified there as "gallegos." In Castón's film, Reme (Mamen Rivera) has become also a kind of pan-Spanish figure whose Galician identity has been subsumed in that "murciana" description made by Peio. It is no wonder, therefore, that Peio ends up calling her "la puta de Oro," meaning both her current physical location and the "gold mine" she represents for all the men in the area, who have quickly taken the position left vacant by yet another absent/present father figure. The fact that Castón has his immigrant worker come from the Cuzco area in Perú, moreover, adds a historical layer in the film's geopolitics. Indeed, few areas and countries in Latin America connote better the sense of lost (colonized) empire than the old site of the powerful Incas and the legendary narratives of "el oro del Perú" (Peru's gold). When Reme stresses that the Basque Country is different to anything else, even, she believes, to that Cuzco where José comes from, she seems to be recalling, simultaneously and unaware of it, the sense of ancient uniqueness, so dear to most Basque tales of origin; and, the fact that the old historical Eldorado, the dream of a rich new home, has now been displaced to this different and improbable location. The "old dream of inhabiting" the father's house, one of the true central tenets of most Basque cinema, is now performed by a Galician mother-prostitute, a neocolonial Peruvian subject, and a homosexual Basque farmer. As conceived by Roberto Castón, a migrant subject himself, the three characters become emblems of the transgression of the heteronormative narrative of the nation while inscribing a trans/postnational space in this new imagined community that emerges in, and seems to make possible, the continuation of the Basque rural way of life. The "casa limpia/clean house" that was Reme's own private dream will no longer be the one belonging to the absent/present father of the old national(ist) narrative. In cinematic terms, however, Castón's opening up of the strict Basque national narrative seems to have found one of the oldest predicaments of Basque cinema in its entirety: its (in)visibility.[51]

It will be that (Basque) cinematic (in)visibility the one that occupies, paradoxically, the narrative center of *Aita*, a film that, as mentioned earlier, is conceived as a non-narrative document of a decayed house that continues to occupy the imaginary center of his inheritor. Like *Ander*, Orbe's film obeys a minimalist aesthetic and is structured through symmetry and repetition. And the most symmetrical of all the repetitions will be precisely the series of spectral projections of the ghosts of the past. These will appear as true moving shadows in the form of the old Basque films used by Orbe to give material texture and historical context to his own spectral refiguration of his father's house. The first of such ghostly projections occurs, precisely, after one of the apparently trivial conversations between Mikel Goneaga, the real local priest of Astigarraga, and Luis Pescador, also the real housekeeper of the Murguia mansion: "Nos dio un susto de muerte…Terminó la oración el muerto!" ("He scared us to death…The deceased ended the prayer!" *Aita.* Film script). The priest is referring to a true event that he witnessed when a man raised his body in the coffin while a prayer was being said for his death. This trivial and quasi humoristic tale of "the living dead" will soon be revisited in real terms by Luis, the old housekeeper, whom we will see leaning against the old walls of the house while the soundtrack produces an old Basque religious hymn. More significantly, the raising of the dead will soon be enacted metafictitiously via the spectral projection of the old Basque films. These will appear during the housekeeper sleepless night because of the combined noise of the storm and the persistent leaks. Luis has stayed in the house because the previous night a few almost invisible young men had broken into it in a robbery attempt. It is significant, in passing, to remark that the only two "visits" of young outsiders to the interior of the house will be this nocturnal robbery and the museum-like visit of a group of local children whose history lesson turns around the age old split of the lords of the land:

> The old lords of Guipuzcoa used to live here. The ancient ones. I am talking about the XIII century. In that time, there were two groups in Guipuzcoa. One were the Oinaztarrak and the other the Gaubautarrak. They were always fighting to have more power...[52]

This didactic form of historical memory will be cinematically compounded by José María de Orbe when he films how two of the girls leave the guided tour to wander on their own. Soon, they will be seen in the darkness of one of the upper rooms and facing each other's terror: "June, let's go. I'm afraid of this!" This entire sequence constitutes the most direct intertextual homage to Víctor Erice's *El espíritu de la colmena* (*The Spirit of the Beehive*, 1973), the masterful spectral conflation of the three (monstruous) absent/present fatherly figures in little Ana's life: that of Franco, the (in)visible yet omnipresent political father; that of her own self-absorbed biological father, the beekeeper played by Fernando Fernán Gómez; and, more importantly, that of Frankenstein, the ultimate cinematic spectral figuration. Orbe's quotation is amplified in the next sequence, where we see Luis donning a mask, quite similar to the one used by the beekeeper in Erice's film, in order to fumigate the noble wood of one of the house relics. What the children's visit establishes, moreover, is the monumental/patrimonial side of the house, whose past is still felt as spectrally present, not only by those terrified girls, but by Luis, the housekeeper, who will confess to the priest that he lives constantly haunted by a white light that follows him anywhere he goes; and, more importantly, by the director and the spectators of the film, who cannot help but fall prey to the spell of this haunted house.

In the film's second spectral cinematic projection, we see images of a child who seems to be also watching us, then we see a young man rising from a bed in exactly the same setting as the housekeeper will duplicate in real life seconds later. This young man appears astonished to see the wall of his room become a kind of cinema screen where barely distinguishable images of old films materialize. The third spectral projection starts with collective images of a beach and a festive *aurresku* (Basque ceremonial dance) and soon repeats the image of the raising young man who witnesses how a small white light takes a human shape and traverses the wall-screen just by his side. The moving shadows will gradually become more recognizable and their cell-like movement in front of a telescopic eye will let us visualize a collectivity in motion, a dancing girl, and an old man clad with a Basque beret smoking. Soon, however, the images will change to show us a burning house and the efforts of a lot of men to put out the fire. The final images will merge the smoke of the burning house with images of the sea and its furious clash against the rocks of the pier. At this point, Orbe seems to be quoting both Basterretxea and Larruquerts' foundational documentary *Ama Lur* (*Mother Earth*, 1968) and Julio Medem's *La pelota vasca. La piel contra la piedra* (*Basque Ball. Skin against Stone*, 2003), the other fundamental documentary film, that Joseba Gabilondo has considered the marker of a new Basque cinema of historical presence.[53] This final spectral projection ends up with a long low angle shot of a white hole surrounded by pitch darkness in what, at first, looks like a nightly shot of the moon, which will gradually become the circular opening of the house inner window that we see now bathed in the whitest of lights. With this Oteizan metaphor, and in the context of this essay, Orbe's ending, just like that of Castón's *Ander*, inscribes an opening up of his familiar narrative enclosure while offering a haunting homage to the spectral persistence of his biological and cinematic forerunners.

Notes

[1]   Giannetti, *Understanding*, 276.

[2]   Ibid., 279.

[3]   Angulo et al., *El cine*, 121 (My emphasis and my translation). Unless indicated, all the translations will be my own.

[4]   The works referred to by Chris Perriam are Bruce Babington's *British Stars and Stardom: From Alma Taylor to Sean Connery* and Richard Dyer's *Heavenly Bodies: Film Stars and Society*.

[5]   Perriam, *Stars*, 8.

[6]   Most recently, in his essay "The National Primal Scene: On Spain's Cinematic Invisibility and the Global Emergence of Basque and Andalusian Cinemas," Joseba Gabilondo has retaken this Freudean figuration to analyze the Spanish constitutional split between Orientalism and Occidentalism as it was already inscribed in Prosper Merimée's novel *Carmen* (1844): "Although the novella *Carmen* has received a great deal of critical attention,…its visual or scopic structure has not been fully analyzed yet —a structure that predates and shapes its later operatic rendition. Although Merimée resorts to the synecdoquic trope of the Gypsy *qua* Andalusian and sets the story in Seville, the focalizing character, the one that gives the point of view to the reader is the Basque don José Lizarrabengoa, who as an old Christian of "pure race" and universal nobility, stands for the French spectator of the drama: Merimée, the author and intradiegetic narrator, as well as his readers. When don José kills Carmen, the former stands for the old occidentalist discourse of Spanish conquest whereas Carmen stands for the orientalist discourse of the othered Spain…Yet,…there is nothing Spanish about *Carmen*: Carmen

and don José are the "others" of Spain and, as "others," stand for an invisible and phantasmatic Spain that emerges from their deadly clash. They ultimately point to a non-Spanish *jouissance* as the foundation of a Spanish primal scene: the inevitable decline of Occidentalism and the deadly seduction of Orientalism. This is the primal scene of Spanish nationalism: the gaze of the Spanish nation is returned by its others, Basques and Andalusians" (Gabilondo, 2011, 1-2). I want to thank Joseba Gabilondo for letting me access this still unpublished manuscript that builds on his earlier essay "On the Inception of Western Sex as Orientalist Theme Park: Tourism and Desire in Nineteenth-Century Spain (*Carmen, Don Juan*)" that was published in *Spain Is (Still) Different: Tourism and Discourse in Spanish Identity*, an anthology that I co-edited with Professor Eugenia Afinoguénova in 2008.

[7] Gabilondo, *Uncanny*, 266-267.

[8] Stone and Jones, "Mapping," 1.

[9] This conference took place from March 30 to April 1, 2011 at The Catalan Center of New York University. I want to thank Professors Miquel A. Pérez-Gómez and Jesús Jiménez-Varea for giving me access to their conclusions and to the film *Ander*.

[10] Pérez-Gómez, "From Tradition," 1.

[11] See "The Dominant Fiction" in Silverman, *Male*, 15-52.

[12] Parker et al., *Nationalisms*, 6.

[13] Parts of this section belong in chapter 6, "Basque Cinema's (Uncanny) Star System" (197-209), in my volume on *Basque Cinema: The Shining Paradox*, currently under consideration by the University of Nevada Press.

[14] Gil de Biedma, "Karra," 57.

[15] Ibid., 59.

[16] Ibid., 59.

[17] Silverman, ibid., 3.

[18] Perriam, ibid., 202.

[19] Etxarri, "Patxi." As Carlos Roldán recalls, Bisquert had just left the prison a short time before the historical events took place: "Con respecto a Patxi Bisquert, él mismo cuenta su participación y su posterior evolución política en una entrevista publicada en *Fotogramas* pocos años después del estreno del film: '...lo que te puedo decir es que yo no estuve en la fuga de la cárcel de Segovia, porque había salido unos meses antes. Estuve en la lucha armada, claro, y en la segunda fuga ayudé currando desde fuera. A partir de la VII Asamblea, cuando el llamado "desdoblamiento", milité en *EIA*, después en *Euskadiko Eskerra,* y al final, por ciertas divergencias, acabé en *Auzolan*" (Roldán, *El cine*, 195).

[20] Abelleira-Briz, "Patxi."

[21] Aizarna, "Tasio."

[22] Armendáriz has been very clear as to his attraction to the real life of those "carboneros," as may be seen by his response to Emma Alonso: "Siempre me han interesado las personas que pasan desapercibidas –dice Montxo– encontré en aquellos hombres una especie de libertad primaria que me fascinó" (Alonso, "Tasio," 45).

[23] Roldán, ibid., 239.

[24] Totoricagüena, *Identity*, 134-135.

[25] V. R. de A, "Xabier."

[26] Perriam, ibid., 15.

[27] Ibid., 25.

[28] See both chapter fours in my volumes *Basque Cinema: An Introduction* and *Basque Cinema: The Shining Paradox*, where parts of this section are developed in further detail.

[29] Parker et al., ibid., 5.

[30] Aretxaga, 1999, 116.

31 Stone and Jones, ibid., 50.

32 For a detailed analysis of this ideological limitation and its recurrence in directors as varied as Juanma Bajo Ulloa or Julio Medem, see my essay, "(M)Otherly Monsters: Old Misogyny and/in New Basque Cinema."

33 Zunzunegui, "El largo viaje," 63-64.

34 Roldán, ibid., 215.

35 Orbe, *Aita* Pressbook.

36 It is interesting to recall here John Hopewell's expressive review: "Pushing even a larger envelope, most of *Ander*'s finance comes from the Basque government, via *Berdindu*, its gay-lesbian service. And the cream of Basque politics—including Basque government president, *Lehendakari* Juan José Ibarretxe—turned out for Ander's world premiere on January 30, when it opened the Basque Country´s *Zinegoak* 09the 6th Bilbao Gay-Lesbian-Trans. Intl. Film Festival, playing to enthusiastic audiences" (Hopwell, *Variety*).

37 Orbe, ibid.

38 Basque cinema's (in)visibility, both in literal and in metaphorical terms, is one of the central arguments in my study *Basque Cinema: The Shining Paradox*.

39 Heredero, *Aita* Pressbook.

40 Silverman, ibid., 4.

41 See Jorge Oteiza's detailed formulation of such a concept (Oteiza, *Quousque*).

42 Gurpegui, "Casa."

43 Salaberria, "José María."

44 Vall, "José María."

45 See, for instance, Mikel Azurmendi´s *La herida patriótica* as a symptomatic use of this metaphor to describe the whole of Euskadi.

46 See my study *Basque Cinema: The Shining Paradox* and, especially, the following passage: "Ultimately, I argue that there are three converging conceptual fields that traverse the Basque Imaginary: the spectral presence of the (violent) past, the *ez/bai* negative affirmation or split id/entity and the migrant condition or the impossible dream of inhabiting/owning the father's house and/or the motherland. Quite often, these conceptual fields produce a common articulation that seems peculiarly Basque. Let us think, for instance, of ETA, doubtlessly the historical referent that has become co-extensive with *Euskadi* in the global media. The armed group, which was born from a historical *split* within the PNB (Nationalist Basque Party), conjured itself by means of violent actions that both haunted and were haunted by the *specter* of State violence and it became *migrant* as its only surviving strategy. Forcing the analogy, one may argue that Basque cinema, as the cultural marker of that id/entity, may be better described if approached in its split, spectral and migrant condition" (Martí-Olivella, *The Shining Paradox*, 6).

47 Ewens, "Ander" (my emphasis).

48 Parker et al., ibid., 6.

49 Such a non-reductive space has been analyzed by Gayatri Spivak in the context of India's tribal bonded prostitution. See her essay "Woman in Difference: Mahasweta Devi's "Duloti the Bountiful" in Parker et al., ibid. I have also studied the symbolic space and the historical reality of forced prostitution as the double limit of the migrant subject position inasmuch as those female sexual workers are placed beyond any legal citizenship and their bodies are, as Spivak refers to them, "encrypted there in the indifference of super-exploitation." (Spivak, "Woman," 113). See Martí-Olivella, "Touristic."

50 *Ander* (Film script).

51 Roberto Castón has complained publically about the apparent impossibility of making his film visible in Spain:

"—¿Sorprendido por no poder estrenar *Ander* en España?—Sí, a estas alturas no sé qué pensar. Llevamos nueve meses con la película de un lado para otro por todo el mundo y aquí no podemos estrenarla. Estuvimos en decenas de festivales internacionales, algunos de ellos de muchísimo prestigio, y recibimos 14 premios internacionales, cuatro de ellos en España. En el Festival de Cine Gay de Madrid, la semana pasada, nos dieron dos premios, el del público y el del jurado. En el festival de Albacete -y no es de temática gay- nos concedieron el galardón a la mejor película, y también en el de Valladolid. Aunque debo decir que los premios más importantes nos los dieron fuera. El festival de Toulouse, donde fueron premiadas películas como *Camino* o *La buena vida*, consideró que *Ander* era la mejor película. En la Berlinale, el pasado febrero, recibimos nuestro primer premio, el de Cines de Arte y Ensayo. Tuvimos también el Premio Lux que da el Parlamento Europeo para destacar los valores sobre los que se asienta la Comunidad Europea...Recibimos críticas estupendas, en revistas extranjeras y en la española *Dirigido por*, pero no encontramos distribución en España, ¿por qué? (Bugallal, "Los dramas").

52   *Aita* (Film script).
53   I am referring to Joseba Gabilondo's already mentioned unpublished manuscript entitled: "The National Prime Scene: On Spain's Cinematic Invisibility and the Global Emergence of Basque and Andalusian cinemas," and, especially, to this paragraph: "Regardless of the 'political content' of [Medem's] film, its approach to Basque reality is radically different from the majority of previous Basque directors and films: it represents Basque reality as politically and historically present." (Gabilondo "Primal Scene," 22).

Bibliography

Abelleira-Briz, José A. "Patxi Bisquert: de la cárcel a actor de moda." *El Diario Vasco* 15 October 1986: 44.

Aita (Pressbook. Eddie Saeta Prod. 2010).

Aizarna, Santiago. "*Tasio*, de Montxo Armendáriz, éxito en el Festival de San Sebastián, en TVE1." *El Diario Vasco* 27 September 1986: 42.

Alonso, Emma. "Tasio o la aventura de un rodaje." *La Voz* 8 July 1985: 45.

Anderson, Benedict. *Imagined Communities: Reflections on the Origin and Spread of Nationalism*. London: Verso, 1983.

Afinoguénova, Eugenia and Jaume Martí-Olivella, eds. *Spain Is (Still) Different: Tourism and Discourse in Spanish Identity*. Lanham, MD: Lexington Books, 2008.

Angulo, Jesús, Carlos F. Heredero and José Luis Rebordinos, eds. *El cine de Imanol Uribe*. Donostia/San Sebastián: Filmoteca Vasca, 1994.

Aretxaga, Begoña. "A Hall of Mirrors: On the Spectral Character of Basque Violence." In *Basque Politics and Nationalism on the Eve of the Millennium,* edited by William A. Douglass, Carmelo Urza, Linda White and Joseba Zulaika, 115-126. Reno: University of Nevada Press, 1999.

Azurmendi, Mikel. *La herida patriótica*. Madrid: Taurus, 1998.

Babington, Bruce. *British Stars and Stardom: From Alma Taylor to Sean Connery*. Manchester: Manchester University Press, 2001.

Bhabha, Homi K. "The Other Question: The Stereotype and Colonial Discourse." In *The Sexual Subject: A Screen Reader in Sexuality,* edited by Stephen Heath, 312-331. London: Routledge, 1999.

Bugallal, Isabel. "Los dramas gay en España sólo triunfan si son de Almodóvar."12 November 2009. *Laopinioncoruña.es*

Dyer, Richard. *Heavenly Bodies: Film Stars and Society.* London/Basingstoke: MacMillan & British Film Institute, 1986.

Etxarri, Tonia. "Patxi Bisquert. Un metalúrgico ex militante de ETA, última revelación del cine vasco." *El Correo Español/El Pueblo Vasco* 15 March 1984: 38.

Ewens, Joseph. "Ander. A Film Review," accessed 05/06/2011, 2011, *DVDoutsider. co.uk/films/reviews/a/ander/.html*

Gabilondo, Joseba. "The National Primal Scene: On Spain's Cinematic Invisibility and the Global Emergence of Basque and Andalusian Cinemas" (Unpublished manuscript).

———. "On the Inception of Western Sex as Orientalist Theme Park: Tourism and Desire in Nineteenth-Century Spain (*Carmen, Don Juan*)." In *Spain Is (Still) Different: Tourism and Discourse in Spanish Identity*, edited by Eugenia Afinoguénova and Jaume Martí-Olivella, 53-87. Lanham: Lexington Books, 2008.

———. "Uncanny Identity: Violence, Gaze, and Desire in Contemporary Basque Cinema." In *Constructing Identity in Contemporary Spain: Theoretical Debates and Cultural Practice*, edited by Jo Labanyi, 262-279. Oxford: Oxford University Press, 2002.

Giannetti, Louis. *Understanding Movie.* 10th edition. Upper Sadle River, NJ: Pearson Education, 2005.

Gil de Biedma, Leticia. "Karra Elejalde. El más duro del cine español." *Man* 1 August 1994: 57-60.

Gurpegui, Mikel G. "Casa Tomada." 24 September 2010. *diariovasco.com*

Heredero, Carlo H. "Misterios de la materia viva" (*Aita*. Pressbook. Eddie Saeta Prod. 2010).

Hopewell, John. "Government Backs *Ander*," accessed 09/02/2011, 2011, www.news.variety.com

Martí-Olivella, Jaume. "(M)Otherly Monsters: Old Misogyny and/in New Basque Cinema." *Anuario de Cine y Literatura en Español* 3 (1997): 89-101.

———. *Basque Cinema: An Introduction.* Reno: Center for Basque Studies. University of Nevada, 2003.

———. "Touristic Trades and Neo-Colonial Subjects." In *Spain Is (Still) Different: Tourism and Discourse in Spanish Identity*, edited by Eugenia Afinoguénova and Jaume Martí-Olivella, 245-267. Lanham, MD: Lexington Books, 2008.

———. *Basque Cinema: The Shining Paradox.* Reno: Center for Basque Studies. University of Nevada (under consideration).

Mosse, George L. *Nationalism and Sexuality: Middle-Class Morality and Sexual Norms in Modern Europe.* Madison, WI: University of Wisconsin Press, 1985.

Oteiza, Jorge. *Quousque Tandem...! Ensayo de interpretación estética del alma vasca.* 5th ed. Iruña/Pamplona: Pamiela, 1994.

Parker, Andrew, Mary Russo, Doris Sommer and Patricia Yaeger, eds. *Nationalisms & Sexualities.* New York and London: Routledge, 1992.

Pérez-Gómez, Miquel, Jesús Jiménez-Varea et al. "From Tradition to the 21st Century. On Basque Men in Film" (unpublished manuscript).

Perriam, Chris. *Stars and Masculinities in Spanish Cinema: From Banderas to Bardem.* Oxford and New York: Oxford University Press, 2003.

Roldán Larreta, Carlos. *El cine del País Vasco: De Ama Lur (1968) a Airbag (1997).* Donostia/San Sebastián: Eusko Ikaskuntza, 1999.

Salaberria, Urkiri. "José María de Orbe Klingenberg/Cineasta." *Zenbukeia 546* (September 2010): 17-24.

Silverman, Kaja. *Male Subjectivity at the Margins.* New York and London: Routledge, 1992.

Spivak, Gayatri. "Woman in Difference: Mahasweta Devi's 'Douloti the Bountiful.'" In *Nationalisms & Sexualities*, edited by Andrew Parker et al., 96-117. New York and London: Routledge, 1992.

Stone, Rob and Helen Jones. "Mapping the Gendered Space of the Basque Country." *Studies in European Cinemas* 1, no 1 (2004): 43-55.

Totoricagüena, Gloria P. *Identity, Culture, and Politics in the Basque Diaspora*. Reno and Las Vegas: University of Nevada Press, 2004.

Vall, Pere. "José María de Orbe: 'Yo no sé si es bueno o malo hacer una película tan difícil de definir.' 10 November 2010: *Fotogramas.es*

V. R. de A. "Xabier Elorriaga." *El Correo Español/El Pueblo Vasco* 20 October 1987: 35.

Zunzunegui, Santos. "El largo viaje hacia la ficción." In *El cine de Imanol Uribe: Entre el documental y la ficción*, edited by Jesús Angulo et al., 53-68. Donostia/San Sebastián: Filmoteca Vasca, 1994.

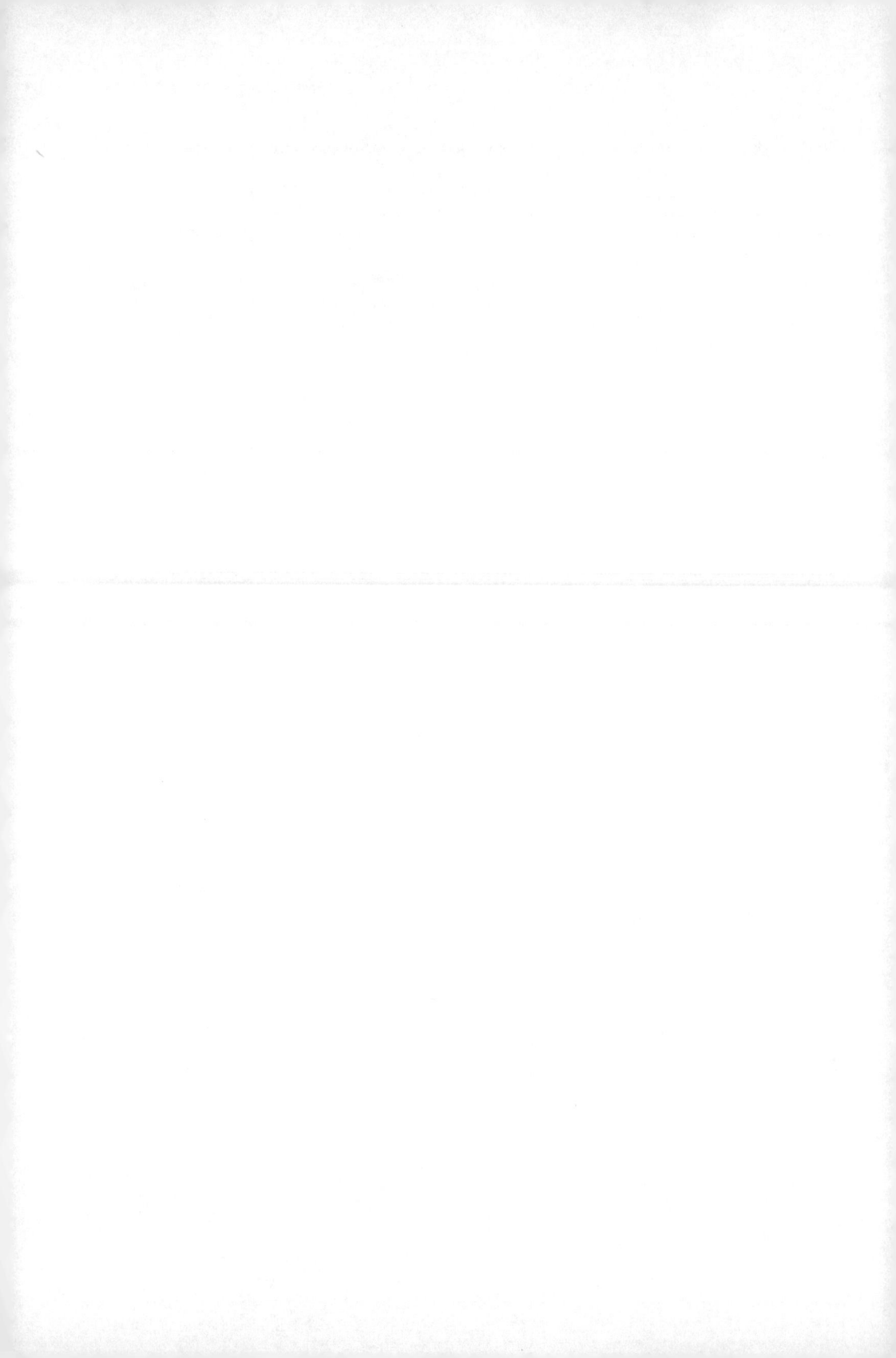

CHAPTER 5

Masculinities in Crisis: A *Tíguere*, a Military Figure, and a *Sanky-panky* as Three Models of Being a Man in the Dominican Republic

Elena Valdez
Rutgers University

In recent years, the ways of conceptualizing masculinity in the Dominican Republic have undergone a significant shift due to multiple changes to the political situation. The presidential elections in 1996 marked the end of the (post-)Trujillo government, and put into crisis the normative masculinity particular to Trujillo's totalitarian regime, whose main representatives were military men and police officers. The 1990s were also the years of the economic restructuring and the growth of the tourism industry in the Dominican Republic, which have become recurrent topics in the recent narrative. Sex tourism perpetuates patterns of economic dependency and stimulates migration based on affectionate relations. Its participants negotiate power through sexuality and contribute to the creation of new identities and configurations of gender, sexuality, and race. In this study, I will address the principal models of Dominican masculinity embodied in a *tíguere*, a *sanky-panky*, and a military male figure. While these are not the only categories for discussing Dominican masculinity, they are ones which are the most emblematic of the crises and changes they have undergone.[1] First, I will explore how these models are interconnected among themselves and transfigured in the twentieth and twenty-first centuries. Second, I will show how the contemporary Dominican narrative sheds light on the complex dynamics of constructing these images of masculinity. I will use the concrete example of how authors Rita Indiana Hernández and Rey Emanuel Andújar produce narratives in which these three models stop being exclusively masculine and heterosexual and begin including ambiguous sexuality.

On *Tígueres*, *Sanky-Pankies*, and Military Figures in the Dominican Republic

The central image of being a man in the Dominican Republic is the *tíguere*, characterized as a Dominican Don Juan, a trickster and a street hustler.[2] The *tíguere* is a person that acts according to the situation. He is both an everyday hero and a trickster, cunning and intelligent, who "gets out of every situation in a manner that is acceptable to others."[3] The word *tíguere* is the Dominican pronunciation of *tigre*, the Spanish word for 'tiger;' it was first used in 1930s in popular sectors of Santo Domingo, the capital of the Dominican Republic. The emergence of the *tíguere*'s masculinity was a reaction to the dictatorial regime of Rafael Leonidas Trujillo, who ruled the country for over 30 years, from 1930 to 1961. The image of the *tíguere* depicts the existence of a particular urban type that readjusted the existing imaginary of masculinity and femininity in the 1930s. Controlled and oppressed by the Trujillo State, ordinary men cultivated "politically innocent activities" in the streets: drinking, dancing, playing dominoes, chasing women.[4] Thus, the image of the *tíguere* is closely linked to its central meaning as the "survivor in his environment,"[5] someone who was trying to evade Trujillo's political repressions.

Further, as Krohn-Hansen explains, the spread of the symbolism of the *tíguere* is also related to the processes of urbanization, migration, and the production of the nation.[6] The formative period of the image of Dominican *tíguere* overlaps with Santo Domingo's transformation into a large city after the hurricane San Zenón that swept the major part of the city on September 3, 1930 and killed approximately 4% of the city's population.[7] The prohibition of internal and external migration in the Dominican Republic during that period and a strong insulation within the margins of the capital became a fertile ground for developing the image of the *tíguere* in the 1940-1950s. In this environment, radio transmissions from Cuba, where the image of the tiger was also prevalent, contributed to the growth of popularity both within the city's limits and in others parts of the country. Also, the maritime-commercial traffic between Cuba and the Dominican Republic reinforced the daily usage of the word.[8] After Trujillo's assassination in 1961, the State restrictions of citizens' movements between rural and urban areas were abolished and the term *tíguere* became fully diffused throughout the country. Nowadays, the *tíguere* has become a fluid identity that is not limited to a strictly masculine gender or a particular social stratum. The word is used in homes and offices, and can be applied to people of different professions (a street trader, public employee, students). It can be used in its diminutive forms as "tiguerito" (my little tiger sons) or an exaggerative one, "ese es un tiguerazo" (the man is a huge *tíguere*). Furthermore, the image and perception of the *tíguere*'s masculinity is being changed under the influence of Dominican Yorks or Dominican Americans. According to Mark Padilla, these imported attitudes have transformed the *tigueraje* into the type that is closely related to the commodity fetishism (the usage of fashionable clothes, brands) and positioned it within the stereotype of the troublemaking *tíguere*.[9]

As many critics have pointed out, [10] the notions of masculinity in the Dominican Republic are mobilized by men's daily life to form relations between themselves, to construct and reinforce their political legitimacy. Collado and Krohn-Hansen,[11] two main researchers of the Dominican *tigueraje*, discuss the manliness of the *tíguere* in terms of set categories: (1) The *tíguere* must be courageous, fearless, and defensive physically and intellectually; (2) he must be publicly visible, that is *dejarse ver*, which draws on the notion of a certain generosity, sharing with the community, willingness to do favors; (3) the *tíguere* is seen as a seducer and a father. The former is a powerful concept of being a Don Juan, womanizer, a nomadic man that is linked to the virility and is recognized by both men and women. Sexual conquest becomes an important part of acting as a *tíguere*, even when a man is married or living in a stable civil union. The latter is a rather contradictory notion of a settled man who must provide for his family, is loyal and supportive, and consequently is closer to the image of the lion, as Antonio de Moya suggests;[12] (4) the *tíguere* should be verbally skillful, communicative, and politically active; (5) the *tíguere* must be sincere and serious. The claim that a person is shameless and insecure can deprive him of the legitimacy. As can be seen, even though the image of the *tíguere* evokes several of these characteristics, it is based on ambiguity. Krohn-Hansen gives a key to comprehending the image of the *tíguere*. The *tíguere*, he explains, is a man who defends himself, knows everything, is seen in the streets and among his friends, uses seductions, and resolve dilemmas, all of which in turn become the source of his ambiguity.[13] The use of the label *tíguere* can either mean approval or disapproval of his behavior. The misconduct, disorder, and disturbance inherent in the term are evident in its employment; sometimes it can characterize the *tíguere* as delinquent or evoke the notion of trickster, and by extension transcend the limitations imposed on acceptable masculinity and shape political legitimacy. The *tíguere* is seen as not completely serious nor as completely negative; dangerous, yet admirable; flexible and programmatic. As pointed out by Krohn-Hansen and Collado, the *tíguere* is part of a national history of political turbulence and terror.[14] Initially, it was forged by ordinary men controlled and oppressed by the Trujillo State, but now it serves to make sense of an imagined Dominican community.[15] In particular, Krohn-Hansen argues that the image of the *tíguere* is in the process of becoming a nationally hegemonic one across the country and abroad.[16]

The second image of masculinity that I analyze in this essay is that of the *sanky-panky*, widely-known in the English-speaking Caribbean as beach boys. The word *sanky-panky* is a linguistic dominicanization of hanky panky. It emerged in the tourist scene of the late 1970s and 1980s with the growth of the presence of young, well-built Dominican men who hustled foreign tourists as a way to make a living. A *sanky-panky*, a Caribbean male sex worker, solicits on tourist-oriented beach areas and has clients of both sexes, primarily white, middle-aged foreign women.[17] The term denotes a particular masculine style; the *sanky pankies* are usually young, black, in good shape, and wear dreadlocks. Their image draws upon cultural and racial stereotypes, and reflects what clients eroticize about these men. As Padilla puts it, they are "'natural' products of an idyllic tropical climate and whose bodies are sculpted by continual exposure to the sea and the Caribbean sun."[18] Even though the vast majority of the encounters with *sanky-pankies* occur on the all-inclusive resorts that scatter the coasts, this is neither to say that all of the men who work at these resorts are *sankies* nor that *sankies* do not exist there and operate outside these resorts. They do not directly negotiate money for sex, but rather prefer to maintain the vision of tourism as that of adventures and romance. Also, as Cabezas explains, direct commercial transactions prevent other possibilities of future financial and emotional gain and confirm an identity as prostitute that they try to resist.[19] They are more likely to create a pseudo-relationship which can be continued through letters, phone calls, faxes, and emails after the guest returns home. They then attempt to ask for money to be sent to them primarily by wire transfer, often using elaborate stories such as sick family members. A *sanky panky*'s ultimate goal is to obtain a marriage visa to the tourist's native country. Even though the *sanky pankies* prefer female tourist clients, male clients are viewed as a more consistent source of income, because they do not require a large time investment in comparison to women.[20] In the same-sex relationship, the *sanky pankies* perform an active (top) role, but they do not identify themselves as homosexual because of social stigmas and sexual behavior. Since they are constantly navigating the border between passivity and activity and always in danger of slipping into *mariconería*, it is important to maintain an "activo reputation" and to deny an engagement with passive sexual acts.[21]

They try to preserve the concordance between their public masculinity and private sexual practices. The marketing of a masculine identity and the usage of their bodies become strategic mechanism to survive in a difficult economic environment.[22] Their masculine bodies become the export commodity on which are placed local and global values, and the *sanky-panky* is a part of what Cabezas calls "sexual commerce."[23] Their gender performance is highly masculine, and they use strategies of discretion, deception, and covering to be seen as *un hombre normal* whose masculinity and sexuality are presumably normative. As Padilla explains, these strategies consist of gender expectations of lower class men who possess a social permissiveness for certain male street activities.[24] Being with foreign clients supposes anonymity since they are not integrated into the *sanky panky*'s social networks, not even when speaking Spanish. Besides this, these encounters attract attention because they are highly public and involve participants from different racial-ethnic and class backgrounds. Thus, by producing a marketable fantasy with their own bodies and gendered performances, the *sanky pankies* play with sexual identities to sell themselves to the clients. According to Padilla, the *sanky panky* is a quintessential *tíguere* of pleasure industry because he exaggerates certain qualities of the *tíguere*'s identities to market their sexual services.[25] The *sanky pankies* perform their identity strategically, moving across different social and sexual spheres; they are both the symbol of male erotic potential and the frequent perpetrators of their promises.

Closely related to a *tíguere* is also the image of totalitarian masculinity represented by military male figures that have to follow a strict code of conduct and can only be involved in a heterosexual relationship. Even though in Latin America the important role in the formation of masculinity and virility traditionally belong to the military school, in the case of the Dominican Republic, the militarization of the country initiated by Rafael Trujillo and continued by the posterior governments extends towards the Dominican society and "militarizes" its culture.[26] The military attitude based on the division of gender, heterosexism, and aggressive homophobia[27] permeates into the daily life of the Dominican society, which initially was already patriarchal, heterosexual, and homophobic.[28] This attitude contributes to the formation of the hegemonic masculinity that emerges, as Raewyn Connell suggests, when "one form of masculinity rather than others is culturally exalted."[29] However, after the presidential election in 1996, the military masculinity experienced crisis and symbolized the end of the era of Trujillo's followers (a so-called new Trujillato). One of the events that triggered such a crisis was the presidential election in 1996 won by Leonel Fernández, who was supported by Joaquín Balaguer, who in turn had been the president of the Dominican Republic three times (1960-1962, 1966-1978 and 1986-1996). Although the results of this victory can bee seen as a new attempt to continue paternalism, it is necessary to recognize it as the end of Balaguer's era and of the new Trujillato.

New Masculinities in Contemporary Dominican Narrative

In this context, the recent Dominican narrative becomes a strategic way to demystify the masculinism and logocentric posture of Trujillo and Balaguer's regimes,[30] which for more than sixty years functioned as a dominant discourse reproduced by ordinary people in everyday life, and that contributed to the political, social, and cultural legitimization in the country.[31] By inserting multiple voices and perspectives, Dominican letters broke away from "monumental knowledge," a certain discursive practice implemented by the governmental system of Trujillo's regime that can be called *Trujillo City*.[32] Thus, the repressed homosexuality of the main character *El Hombre Triángulo* (2005) by Rey Emmanuel Andújar becomes a metaphor for a decaying institutionalized military masculinity that is no longer capable of sustaining itself unless it turns to corruption. The masculinity in crisis of the main character is a trope that allows intervening into the dominant monophonic discourse and channeling queer voices towards a new polyphonic one. *La estrategia de Chochueca* (2000) by Rita Indiana Hernández challenges Trujillo and Balaguer's masculinism from at least two perspectives, that of femininity and sexual ambiguity. Revealing a feminine experience of cruising in the city and enjoying homoerotic pleasure, the main protagonist of Hernández's novel distances herself from the gender expectations imposed by society at the same time as she questions the invariability of sexual identities. Her sexually ambiguous conduct becomes a metaphor for a nation that is about to define its future after a long period of dictatorships.

The Triangle Man (2005) by Rey Emmanuel Andújar is a novel about Pedro Pérez, the police lieutenant. One day, Pérez interrogates Baraka, nicknamed the triangle man, because of his ambiguous sexuality, although he is later allowed to leave freely. Pérez is mourning the death of his child, and his own reclusion in the mental hospital of Matilda, with whom he had a brief intimate relationship. While subsequently frequenting bars, Pérez meets Baraka, and after drunkenly confessing his sufferings, Baraka kisses him. In response, Pérez hits Baraka and runs home to commit suicide; Baraka leaves town. Saved by one of his neighbors, Pérez visits Rotunda, a prostitute who tells him about her decision to leave the country and work in the Netherlands. Pérez bursts out crying desperately. Not knowing how to console him, Rotunda penetrates him anally with her fingers giving the lieutenant great pleasure.

The Triangle Man presents the crisis of the normative masculinity that supposes the crossing of military attitudes and a traditionally macho culture associated with patriarchy, heterosexuality, and heteronormativity. Firstly, the novel demystifies the military education that is under the foreign influence.[33] The military school where Pérez goes propagates a white masculinity as a hegemonic one through U.S. war and adventure movies. Alien to the Dominican context and to its history of miscegenation,[34] this hegemonic masculinity prevents its own production and triggers Pérez's future failure of becoming a real man, since he is not white himself.

Secondly, his demeanor does not correspond to the traditional image of a virile man. In order to look more virile, he grows a beard, but his voice is somewhat "between military and melodious" and this seemingly minor detail does not coincide with one of the parameters of a "real man's" behavior.[35] In this context his name has a certain symbolism. Pedro is clearly associated with the word "piedra" (stone), a hard material, difficult to break. As the name suggests, Pérez personifies an image of implacable masculinity and a masculine body as the phallus. According to Michael Kaufman, masculinity is also based on how power and control are exercised,[36] which can be seen mainly in the way Pérez speaks. The use of coarse language characterizes him as a man, being another attribute of an acceptable masculine behavior, according to de Moya.[37] For example, Pérez swears throughout the whole novel: "Me cago en Ceuta, cuando coño le van a dejar la vida en paz a uno en este destacamento" [Damn, when the fuck they will leave him in peace in this police station];[38] "¿qué-mierda-es-eso?" [What is this shit?];[39] "eso me encojona" [It is pissing me off.][40] His speech reveals this logocentric posture that is part of the system of masculine domination and that reinforces gender politics.[41]

Thirdly, I would like to extend Rafael Ramírez's studies of Puerto Rican masculinity into my analysis of Andújar's novel. According to this Puerto Rican scholar, Pérez's manliness needs to be seen and recognized by others.[42] However, in the novel there are two moments when Pérez's masculinity is undermined. First, the attitude of his co-workers appears to be ambiguous because they do not see him as *tíguere* when, for example, his boss, lieutenant Rojas, says: "Usted luce cansado, tigre, póngase en órbita, deje de beber, deje la parranda, que ya me han contado" [You look tired, tíguere, pull yourself together, stop drinking, stop partying, as they have told me.][43] Second, the event that reduces his manliness is a relationship with his girlfriend. As Ramírez points out, to satisfy a woman is important in order to maintain the virile image because an unsatisfied woman is a potential adulteress.[44] Thus, when Pérez's girlfriend cheats on him, he does not defend his honor and consequently does not receive a homosocial approval of his friends and neighbors.[45] He thus becomes a person who in the Dominican Republic is called "the defiling stigma of a cuckold, a synonym of abjection, of being an outcast."[46]

Next, the fact that he is not seen as a father and breadwinner also reduces his masculinity. De Moya explores the dual nature of the manliness because men are able to circulate within two worlds, the house and the street, maintaining the monopoly of the last.[47] In terms of a domestic life, Pérez at first glance seems to correspond to the normative masculine image. The only intimate heterosexual relationship acceptable, according to Gayle Rubin's presentation of "good" and "bad" sex,[48] is the relationship between Matilda and Pérez when they conceive a child. But the act of having a child does not legitimize Pérez's masculinity. In his study of Mediterranean masculinities, Gilmore explains that "the image of masculinity confers respect to its carrier and security to his family, lineage or people, since these groups, by sharing a collective identity, reflect the reputation of the man and this reputation protects him."[49] Even though Pérez has a child, he does not fulfill his paternal duty. The community notices this attitude and reproaches him when he does not react or cry during the funeral service after the death of his child; in the eyes of the community, he is not seen as a father.

Pérez fails even as a womanizer. The domestic environment created with Matilda and Pérez's relationship is dissolved with private encounters that take place between the lieutenant and Rotunda, a very masculine prostitute:

she has hairs on her legs, natural small moustache, and harsh voice. Rotunda is characterized by the residual masculinity, a category defined by de Moya and used to refer to "'mannish' females (not necessarily lesbians), virilized by attitudes, hormones or medication, stereotypically regarded and treated by hegemonic males as males or 'social men.'"[50] For Pérez, Rotunda becomes this "social man," a companion with whom he talks; it is even said that Rotunda knows more than the police chief himself. In comparison to her, Pérez appears more feminine. On the one hand, Rotunda treats Pérez in a very motherly fashion. He is infantilized during his first encounter with the prostitute, while Rotunda's actions make her out to be a maternal figure. She undresses him as if he was a child; she washes his genitals, listens to him attentively and puts him to bed. Pérez's masculinity stops being hegemonic and is reduced to a subordinated one because, according to Nurse, subordinated masculinity is presented as infantile.[51] On the other hand, Pérez fails during the sexual conquest, which is important for the construction of a virile mage. Impressed by meeting Baraka, he cannot get an erection and, thus, is unable to perform his masculine obligations: "decía Pérez, esperando que por favor se le parara, con un condón en la mano" [Pérez was saying, wishing that he would get it up, with a condom in his hand.][52] This scene points out, according to Martínez San-Miguel, Pérez's incapacity to accept his homosexuality.[53] Rotunda is thus a multifaceted character who represents the failure of Pérez's masculine image, his homosexual preferences, and the impossibility to accept them openly. In the end of the novel, when Pérez finds out about Rotunda's decision to leave the country for the Netherlands, he starts behaving hysterically, a conduct associated with women: "Rotunda no tenía miedo pero nunca había visto a Pérez así, llorando, tirado en el piso babeando con un llanto que le salía de alguna constelación en el pecho desnudo que golpeaba con un puño cada vez que hablaba" [Rotunda was not scared, but she had never seen Pérez like this, crying, lying on the floor, drooling with a cry that was escaping from some constellation in his naked chest that he was hitting with a fist every time he spoke.][54] This kind of behavior destroys the vision of a masculine body as the phallus (such as the name Pedro suggested): it is not erected, pure muscle anymore, but rather is thrown to the floor shaking. Besides, Rotunda's decision to go to the Netherlands can be seen as a challenge to the sexual order. Questioning the idea that women depend on men financially further reduces Pérez's virility and manliness, and depicts the dissolution of a traditional family.

The appearance of Baraka's character undermines Pérez's masculinity even more because it reveals his repressed homosexuality. The first sign of this appears during their first encounter, when Pérez interrogates Baraka. The latter destroys the hierarchy that exists between the military personnel and the other men, when he answers Pérez's questions and turns to using coarse language to challenge the military logocentric order: "Todos los días son una esperanza orgánica, pendejo" [Every day is an organic hope, jackass.][55] "To see an effeminate man," as Elisabeth Badinter explains, "arouses a dreadful anxiety in many men; it makes them aware of their own feminine characteristics, such as passivity or sensitivity, which they consider to be a sign of weakness".[56] Therefore, Baraka's presence and his ambiguous sexuality conducts the process of Pérez's identification with him, revels Pérez's double life and personality, his repressed homosexual tendencies and fear of accepting them openly. Pérez silences his emerging sexuality because being a military man he must maintain his virile image and be recognized as such, all of which constitutes his experience of closetedness.[57] Foucault insists on the importance of knowing how to interpret such a silence surrounding the sexual, because these ways of "not saying" are strategies that make clear human sexuality.[58] Thus, Baraka becomes the only character who knows how to read Pérez's silence: "Sé que sufres, se te nota, tienes un tormento, pero eres mucho más que eso...Un hombre solo y sin consuelo, complicado, pero bueno, y creo que puedo quererte..." [I know that you are suffering, it's noticeable, you have a torment, but you are much more than this...A lonely man without consolation, complicated, but good, and I think I can love you...][59]

The key moment in this process is the second encounter between Pérez and Baraka that takes place in the bar Parada 77, a real place in Santo Domingo famous for its gay environment. In this very moment Baraka transforms into Pérez's double: "Pérez veía al Hombre Triángulo sufrir y era como mirarse en un espejo" [Pérez saw the triangle man suffer and it was like seeing yourself in a mirror.][60] It turns out that Baraka is not only Pérez' double, but also represents his repressed homosexual desire, which does not allow him to find a place for his own in a binary world stricken by the multigenerational implementation of a militarized and homophobic culture in Santo Domingo. This way, Baraka recognizes himself in Pérez, and that is why he hugs him first and insists on kissing him. In response, Pérez hits him, which turns out to be an act caused by the homosexual masculine panic[61] whereby he attempts to maintain his image of manliness with violence, to sustain his dominance: "Coño, qué es eso, un hombre besando a un guardia... Machismo en toda extensión de la palabra" [Fuck, what is this, a man kissing a guard... machismo in every sense of the word.][62] As Gregory Herek explains, the homophobia fulfills a social function when a heterosexual man expresses his prejudices against the homosexual to obtain the approval of the others and to increase his own confidence.[63] As it turns out, the man is opposed to the guard; in turn this opposition once again reveals the dominant position of military masculinity incompatible with homosexual practices. Later, Baraka describes Pérez as a coward: "cobardía de macharrán."[64] As de Moya explains, the word "macharrán" belongs to the groups of labels that are used to describe hegemonic masculinities in everyday life. This word supposes that a man is exclusively heterosexual, has multiple women and children from different women that he fails to support.[65] Hitting Baraka, Pérez does not try to establish his manliness, but instead realizes the impossibility of achieving it. Therefore, he does not have another solution than to commit suicide; the suicide becomes a gendered act, an act traditionally ascribed to women, which once and for all annihilates his masculinity.[66]

Chochueca's Strategy by Rita Indiana Hernández, on the other hand, is constructed as a series of walks by Silvia, the main character of the novel, whose main objective is to return stolen speakers either to their owner or to the police. Accompanied by her friend Tony, Silvia fulfills her promise. The novel reconstructs sharp observations of urban reality and reflects the generational boredom of the youth of the nineties. Through Silvia's wanderings, the city of Santo Domingo is depicted as a previously unknown territory of invisible youth culture, of drugs, of street violence, and explicit sexual acts that took place between herself and some of her friends from different social classes: Salim, Octaviano, Julia and Amanda. The novel ends with Silvia visiting Franco, her homosexual friend, at the hospital.

In his book *Escrituras de desencuentro en la República Dominicana*, Rodríguez writes that "in *Chochueca's Strategy* the history distances itself a lot from being the substantially fundamental element in the configuration of the ideal for homeland that, as the logic of the city Trujillo prescribes, is supposed to be assimilated by the individuals as irrefutable principle."[67] This logic of Trujillo's city is based on what Jacqueline Jiménez Polanco calls "the exclusion of the heterogeneity from the space of the public" in order to conceive the nation as "a constitutional homogeneous, hierarchical and stately unit."[68] Even though Rodriguez mainly explores the urban space of

Santo Domingo, I would like as a point of departure to refer to both Dominican scholars to illustrate how the monolithic and solid urban space is destroyed (and as a consequence other structures and institutions), and how the heterogeneity is reinscribed into the conception of the nation. Thus, I am interested in showing how in the beginning of the twentiety-first century the strict division between public and private places is destroyed and how a fragmented environment is being created that allows the consequent erruption of ambiguous sexuality into the urban landscape.

The relocations within the city of Santo Domingo become for Silvia a place of enunciation, asconceptualized by de Certeau.[69] In the streets she seems to follow the logic of the *flâneur* as an observer.[70] At the same time, she is not the indolent *flâneur* of Walter Benjamin with his distant and aesthetic look, but a perceptive *flâneuse* who is obliged to unmask and criticize society's evil, to reveal that the dominant discourse stops being masculine and obtains a feminine and sexually ambiguous voice. While walking, she is usually accompanied by one of her male friends, which seems to reproduce the nineteenth-century image of a *flâneuse* who must be accompanied in public spaces. In spite of this, in *Chochueca's Strategy* the traditional roles that every couple must follow in public places are destroyed. Even though Silvia goes all over Santo Domingo with Tony or Salim, she is not a woman who follows a man. Rather, it is she who chooses which way to go, establishes her own conduct, and becomes a figure that channels new ways to inhabit the city: to wander for the sake of wandering. Additionally, she comments a Caribbean way of walking disassociated from politics, a way of walking the nation. The narrator says: "La sola acción de andar ofrece posibilidades inevitables, se camina sin pensar que se camina, más bien tinteamos las caderas acompasando las piernas a la cadencia autómata" [The only act of walking offers inevitable possibilities, you are walking without thinking that you walking, rather jingling with your hips keeping your legs in time with automatic rhythm.][71] In this context, the wanderings of the main character have another symbolism in the novel. Her interminable walks represent the lack of place for the nation, above all when Silvia describes the same relocations of Santo Domingo's inhabitants as "el infame cabalgar de la gente, gente sola que no va a ninguna parte" [the dreadful riding of people, lonely people who go nowhere.][72]

What becomes even more important is that this hybrid urban space destroys hierarchies and divisions that preserved gender roles. Through her way of walking, the protagonist articulates her own place in the world and a new way of practicing the city. All the surfaces of Santo Domingo function as a counter-public sphere which, according to the definition of Rita Felski, solidifies the opposition to the discrimination and oppression by the predominantly masculine culture, disseminates ideas and values, and puts emphasis on the feminine experience.[73] In Hernández's novel, the counter-public sphere of the Dominican capital is not based exclusively on issues of gender, but also introduces ambisexual explorations of the city dwellers' environment. While walking, Silvia does not only appropriate urban space, but also the public urban space traditionally ascribed to the men: she is a new street hustler, a *tíguere*, a traditionally masculine identity, and embodies his main features. In the novel, Silvia is able to enter the streets as a place of socializing and as an initiation to manliness; she becomes coarse, a behavior traditionally seen as a masculine attribute. Nor is she afraid of returning the speakers.

In this context, the new urban space destroys gender hierarchies for other characters as well. The street becomes a locus for scandals based on the sexual; for example, when Tony's girlfriend hits him and makes him cry, Silvia remains calm and thus is depicted as more masculine: "Tony estaba histérico con las bocinas, yo no, yo cantaba feliz de mi Cocacola y de mi Bjork con hielo, sintiéndome como una princesa del bien" [Tony was hysterical with the speakers, and I ain't, I was singing happy with my Cocacola and Bjork with ice, feeling as a rich princess.][74] Other male characters are presented as more cowardly and more feminized, while Silvia appropriates their space and masculine role of dominating the streets. For example, in one scene when Silvia asks Manuel to help her to return the speakers, he is about to start crying, while Silvia keeps insisting, like a *tíguere* who will not quit, until she gets what she wants. Silvia also comments on the political and social situations in the country, is promiscuous and able to trespass gender boundaries and have same-sex relationships. The protagonist of Silvia embodies the *tíguere*'s ambiguity because she can be seen as a person who helps her friends and at the same time acts as a criminal, stigmatized for her improper social and sexual conduct. As a result, what was previously considered a nationally hegemonic model of masculinity, as Krohn-Hansen defines it,[75] starts to incorporate other subjectivities. Following this masculine model, Silvia inherits a reaction against Trujillo's political regime, as implied by this image. But, in the beginning of the twenty-first century, this challenge consists of breaking with the patriarchal posture of exclusion, and of including the ambiguous sexuality which was previously disassociated from the *tigueraje* as a national identity.

Sexual tourism is not a central theme in the novel, but rather a background that emerges through Silvia's comments while she is walking the streets of Santo Domingo with Salim. Supposedly, he is a sexual worker who is involved with a group of Scandinavian tourists and has relationships only with women of a stable financial standing. As Silvia comments, "cuando andábamos las calles a pie, la gente siempre tan necia y poco delicada, probablemente pensaba, 'mira esa pobre gringuita cayó en las manos de ese sanki'" [While we walked the streets, the foolish and insensitive people were always probably thinking, 'look, this poor American fell into that sanki's hands.']⁷⁶ It is interesting that Silvia is aware of this image and subverts it on purpose, since all *sankies'* actions and conducts are public and include participants of different classes and racial-ethnic origins. Silvia comments: "por eso cuando cruzábamos cortando tumultos en las aceras y la gente se volteaba a mirar a la blanquita y al negro, yo subía la voz como un carro de bomberos, con un acento capitaleño que dejaba flaco al de cualquier tigre de Villas Agrícola..." [That's why when we were cutting through the commotion on the sidewalks and the people were turning to look at the white woman and a black man, I used to raise my voice like a fire truck, with a capital accent that left terrified any tiger from Villa Agricola.]⁷⁷ Silvia not only destroys the image ascribed to her with its racial characteristics of a white, passive, submissive tourist-victim who is looking for pleasure with a black Dominican *sanky panky*, but instead takes command of a masculine language and claims her own place within the public urban space. By raising her voice, Silvia undermines the production of a commercialized fantasy that Salim presents with his body and masculine gender performance in order to sell it to the clients.

As can be seen, both *The Triangle Man* and *Chochueca's Strategy* suggest an intervention into Dominican society and culture, which continue being patriarchic, heterosexual and heteronormative, and stigmatize queer relationships. Both texts are part of what Rodriguez calls "the counter-narrative of Trujillo City"⁷⁸ and demystify the paternalist masculine discourse of Trujillo's regime. The battlefield is the city of Santo Domingo. Constant relocations of main characters within the urban space put into crisis their virile and feminine images, problematize their sexuality, and transform them into sexually ambiguous beings. Their precarious identities enable them to permeate into the subaltern underworld and witness the growth of the queer population in the Dominican Republic. Being liminal characters, they are symptomatic of the crisis of a world in transformation and embody tensions and difficulties of this liminal position that the Dominican Republic occupies. Consequently, an ambiguous sexuality becomes a trope to talk about the political, cultural, sexual, and national complexity of a country that has suffered a dictatorship for sixty years and, at the moment of the publication of both texts, has been defining its future path.

Notes

[1] For an excellent overview of different masculinities in the Dominican Republic, see de Moya, "Power Games," 68-104; and Padilla, *Caribbean*.

[2] Collado, *El tíguere*, 25.

[3] Krohn-Hansen, "Masculinity," 109.

[4] Krohn-Hansen, ibid., 127; and Collado, ibid., 34.

[5] Krohn-Hansen, ibid., 108.

[6] Ibid., 125.

[7] Derby, *The Dictator*'s, 66.

[8] Collado, ibid., 24.

[9] Padilla, ibid., 71.

[10] For a good presentation of the mobilization of the notions of masculinity in a daily life, see de Moya, "Power Games," 68-72; and Krohn-Hansen, "Masculinity," 108-111.

[11] Collado, ibid., 125-158; and Krohn-Hansen, ibid., 112-120.

[12] de Moya, ibid., 80.

[13] Krohn-Hansen, ibid., 121.

[14] Ibid., 127.

[15] Ibid., 127.

[16] The image of the *tíguere* has been commonly addressed in the works of Dominican and Dominican American authors. Some examples include the short stories by Junot Díaz and his acclaimed novel *The Brief and Wondrous Life of Oscar Wao*, where Oscar and Yunor, the two main characters, represent a problematic correspondence and relation to the model of normative masculinity.

[17] Cabezas, "Between," 995.

[18] Padilla, ibid., 19.

[19] Cabezas, ibid., 999.

[20] Padilla, "The Embodiment," 787.

[21] Padilla, *Caribbean*, 96.

[22] Padilla, "The Embodiment," 785.

[23] Cabezas, ibid., 988.

[24] Padilla, ibid., 785.

[25] Padilla, *Caribbean*, 134.

[26] In the Dominican Republic, the Cuban Revolution in 1959 created an environment of tension and anxiety because Rafael Leonidas Trujillo ended up being one of the few Latin American dictators and was afraid of the invasion of Dominicans who lived in exile in Cuba and Venezuela (Hall, *Sugar*, 89). According to Michael Hall, the government increased military investments, acquisition of military amenities abroad, and promoted recruitment into the army. In addition to the military budget of 1959 that consisted of 38.7 millions dollars, Trujillo added 50 millions more for an immediate acquisition of

weapons and the maintenance of the Dominican Army that already counted 25000 persons. Thus, between 1930 and 1960 Rafael Leonidas Trujillo had the largest army in the region (Hall, *Sugar*, 105). Moreover, the army and military elite played an important role in Dominican politics in the second half of the 20th century: during Joaquín Balaguer's ascension to power; during the presidency of Antonio Guzmán and the military oligarchy that forced Balaguer to withdraw his candidate from the vice-presidential election; and during the army restructuring by Jorge Blanco (Moya-Pons, *The Dominican*, 381-420).

[27] Morgan, "Theater," 166-168.

[28] For general studies about homophobia in the Dominican society, see Horn ("Queer," 372); Espinosa-Miñoso ("Homogeneidad," 364-366). In spite of this, we cannot dismiss the cultural production and critical studies about Dominican queer sexuality both in the island and the Diaspora, as studied by Jacqueline Jiménez-Polanco, Antonio de Moya, Mark Padilla, and Carlos Decena, among others. In particular, it is necessary to bring out *Divagaciones bajo la luna*, a volume of lesbian poetry compiled by Jiménez-Polanco in 2006, and the first *Antología gay dominicana* (2004), which provoked various debates and controversies. Also, we can mention the work of activists groups that defend human rights and promote integral health among Dominic LGBT community: ReVASA (Red de voluntarios de ASA) and Transsa (Trans Siempre Amigas).

[29] Connell, *Masculinities*, 76-77.

[30] Keith Nurse writes that "masculinism, as the hegemonic ideational construct, achieves a *logocentric* posture" ("Masculinities," 7).

[31] de Moya, ibid., 70.

[32] Rodríguez, *La Isla*, 17.

[33] The Dominican Republic possesses a long history and tradition of a military education that even nowadays is considered a privileged occupation. One of the examples can be the publication of the book about La Academia Militar "Batalla de las Carreras" written by its cadets Sención Silverio and Freites Báez in 2006.

[34] In the twentieth century was solidified the politics of whitening, embraced by the concept of the *hispanidad* and promoted by the State machine (Rodríguez, ibid., 10-11). The Trujilliato and new Trujilliato took possession of the real and discursive formation of Dominican racial and national identity. For more information on the whitening in the Dominican Republic, see Howard; Matibag; Stinchcomb; Torres-Saillant; and Simmons, among others.

[35] Andújar, *The Triangle Man,* 12.

[36] Kaufman, "Las experiencias," 63.

[37] de Moya, ibid., 74.

[38] Andújar, ibid.,12.

[39] Ibid., 13.

[40] Ibid., 17.

[41] Connell, ibid., 83.

[42] Ramírez, What, 33.

[43] Andújar, ibid., 17.

[44] Ramírez, ibid., 46.

[45] "Homosocial approval" is a term coined by Michael Kimmel ("Homofobia," 54-55).

[46] de Moya, ibid., 69.

[47] Ibid., 77.

[48] Rubin, "Thinking Sex," 14.

[49] Gilmore, "Cuenca," 83.

[50] de Moya, ibid., 81.

[51] Nurse, ibid., 7.

52   Andújar, ibid., 28.
53   Martínez-San Miguel, 1052.
54   Andújar, ibid., 63.
55   Ibid., 22.
56   Badinter, *XY*, 116.
57   Sedgwick, *Epistemology*, 3.
58   Foucault, *History*, 27.
59   Andújar, ibid., 22.
60   Ibid., 45.
61   Sedgwick defines the notion of "homosexual panic" in the following way: "The most private, psychologized form in which many twentieth-century western men experience their vulnerability to the social pressure of homophobic blackmail; even for them, however, that is only one path to control, complementary to public sanctions through the institutions described by Foucault and others as defining and regulating the amorphous territory of the 'sexual'" (*Between*, 89).
62   Andújar, ibid., 50.
63   Herek, "On Heterosexual," 569.
64   Andújar, ibid., 54.
65   de Moya, ibid., 83.
66   Suicide appears as a motif of the death of the homosexual man in Latin American narrative. Another such text that presents this motif, for example, is *El ángel de Sodoma* (1928) by Alfonso Hernández Catá.
67   Rodríguez, Escrituras, 142-143.
68   Jiménez-Polanco, "Las mujeres," 315.
69   de Certeau, *The* Practice, 97-98.
70   Ibid., 40-41.
71   Hernández, *Chochueca's Strategy*, 10.
72   Ibid., 31.
73   Felski, Beyond, 167.
74   Hernández, ibid., 47.
75   Krohn-Hansen, ibid., 127.
76   Hernández, ibid., 21.
77   Ibid., 21.
78   Rodríguez, *Escrituras*, 143.

Bibliography

Andújar, R. Emmanuel. *El Hombre Triángulo*. San Juan, P.R.: Editorial Isla Negra, 2005.
Badinter, Elisabeth. *XY: On Masculine Identity*. New York: Columbia University Press, 1995.
Cabezas, Amalia. "Between Love and Money: Sex, Tourism, and Citizenship in Cuba and the Dominican Republic." *Signs* 29, no. 4 (2004): 987-1015.
Collado, Lipe. *El tíguere dominicano: hacia una aproximación de cómo son los dominicanos*. Santo Domingo, Rep. Dominicana: Editora Collado, 2002.
Connell, Raewyn. *Masculinities*. Berkeley: University of California Press, 1995.
de Certeau, Michel. *The Practice of Everyday Life*. Berkeley: University of California Press, 1988.
de Moya, Antonio. "Power Games and Totalitarian Masculinity in the Dominican Republic." In *Interrogating Caribbean Masculinities: Theoretical and Empirical Analyses*, edited by Rhoda Reddock, 68-104. Kingston, Jamaica: University of the West Indies Press, 2004.

Decena, Carlos Ulises. *Tacit Subjects: Belonging and Same-Sex Desire among Dominican Immigrant Men.* Durham N.C.: Duke University Press, 2011.

Derby, Lauren H. *The Dictator's Seduction. Politics and the Popular Imagination in the Era of Trujillo.* Durham and London: Duke University Press, 2009.

Díaz, Junot. *The Brief Wondrous Life of Oscar Wao.* New York: Riverhead Books, 2007.

———. *Drown.* New York: Riverhead Books, 1996.

Espinosa-Miñoso, Yuderkys. "Homogeneidad, proyecto de nación y homofobia." In *Desde la orilla hacia una nacionalidad sin desalojos,* edited by Silvio Torres-Saillant, Ramona Hernández and Blas Jiménez, 361-368. Santo Domingo: Editora Manatí, Ediciones Librería La Trinitaria, 2004.

Felski, Rita. *Beyond Feminist Aesthetics: Feminist Literature and Social Change.* Cambridge, Mass: Harvard University Press, 1989.

Foucault, Michel. *The History of Sexuality.* Translated by Robert Hurley. Vol. 1. New York: Vintage Books, 1990.

García, Mélida and Miguel de Camps Jiménez. *Antología De La Literatura Gay En La República Dominicana.* 1st ed. Santo Domingo, República Dominicana: Editora Manatí, 2004.

Gilmore, D. D. "Cuenca mediterránea: la excelencia en la actuación." In *Masculinidades, Poder y Crisis,* edited by T. Valdés y J. Olavarría, 82-101. Santiago, Chile: Ediciones de las Mujeres no 24, Isis Internacional/FLACSO, 1997.

Hall, Michael R. *Sugar and Power in the Dominican Republic: Eisenhower, Kennedy, and the Trujillos.* Westport, Conn.: Greenwood Press, 2000.

Herek, Gregory M. "On Heterosexual Masculinity. Some Physical Consequences of the Social Construction of Gender and Sexuality." *American Behavioral Scientist* 29, no. 5 (1986): 563-577.

Hernández Catá, Alfonso. *El Ángel de Sodoma.* Madrid: Mundo latino, 1928.

Hernández, Rita Indiana. *La Estrategia de Chochueca.* Santo Domingo: Riann Editorial, 2000.

Howard, David John. *Coloring the Nation: Race and Ethnicity in the Dominican Republic.* Oxford, U.K; Boulder, Co.: Signal Books, L. Rienner Publishers, 2001.

Horn, Maja. "Queer Caribbean Homecomings. The Collaborative Art Exhibits of Nelson Ricart-Guerrero and Christian Vauzelle." *GLQ* 14 (2008): 361-381.

Jiménez-Polanco, Jacqueline. *Divagaciones Bajo La Luna : Voces e Imágenes de Lesbianas Dominicanas* [Musings Under the Moon : Voices and Images of Dominican Lesbians]. Santo Domingo and New York: Idegraf Editora, 2006.

———. "Las mujeres y otros subordinados en el espacio público nacional." In *Desde la orilla hacia una nacionalidad sin desalojos,* edited by Silvio Torres-Saillant, Ramona Hernández and Blas Jiménez, 315-332. Santo Domingo: Editora Manatí, Ediciones Librería La Trinitaria, 2004.

Kaufman, Michael. "Las experiencias contradictorias del poder entre los hombres." In *Masculinidades, Poder y Crisis,* edited by T. Valdés y J. Olavarría, 63-81. Santiago, Chile: Ediciones de las Mujeres no 24, Isis Internacional/FLACSO, 1997.

Kimmel, Michael S. "Homofobia, temor, vergüenza y silencio en la identidad masculina." In *Masculinidades, Poder y Crisis,* edited by T. Valdés y J. Olavarría, 49-62. Santiago, Chile: Ediciones de las Mujeres no 24, Isis Internacional/FLACSO, 1997.

Krohn-Hansen, Christian. "Masculinity and the Political among Dominicans: 'The Dominican Tiger.'" In *Machos, Mistresses, Madonnas,* edited by Marit Melhuus and Kristi Ann Stølen, 108-133. London and New York: Verso, 1996.

Martínez-San Miguel, Yolanda. "Más allá de la homonormatividad: intimidades alternativas en el Caribe hispano." *Revista Iberoamericana* 25 (2008): 1039-1057.

Matibag, Eugenio. *Haitian-Dominican Counterpoint: Nation, State, and Race on Hispaniola.* New York: Palgrave, 2003.

Morgan, David. "Theater of War. Combat, the Military, and Masculinities." In *Theorizing Masculinities*, edited by Harry Brod and Michael Kaufman, 165-181. Thousand Oaks, CA, London and New Delhi: Sage, 1994.

Moya-Pons, Frank. *The Dominican Republic: A National History*. Princeton, N.J: Markus Wiener Publishers, 1998.

Nurse, Keith. "Masculinities in Transition: Gender and the Global Problematique." In *Interrogating Caribbean Masculinities: Theoretical and Empirical Analyses*, edited by Rhoda Reddock, 3-37. Kingston, Jamaica: University of the West Indies Press, 2004.

Padilla, Mark. "The Embodiment of Tourism among Bisexually-Behaving Dominican Male Sex Workers." *Archives of Sexual Behavior* 37 (2008):783–793.

———. *Caribbean Pleasure Industry: Tourism, Sexuality, and AIDS in the Dominican Republic*. Chicago: University of Chicago Press, 2007.

Ramírez, Rafael L. and Rosa E. Casper. *What it Means to be a Man: Reflections on Puerto Rican Masculinity*. New Brunswick, NJ: Rutgers University Press, 1999.

Rodríguez, Néstor E. *Escrituras de Desencuentro en la República Dominicana*. Mexico D.F: Siglo XXI, 2005.

———. *La Isla y su envés: Representaciones de lo nacional en el ensayo dominicano contemporáneo*. 1st ed. San Juan, P.R: Instituto de Cultura Puertorriqueña, 2003.

Rubin, Gayle S. "Thinking Sex: Notes for a radical Theory of the Politics of Sexuality." In *The Lesbian and Gay Studies Reader*, edited by Henry Abelove, Michele Aina Barale, David M. Halperin, 3-44. New York, London: Routledge, 1993.

Sanky panky. 1 videodisc: sd., col.; 4 3/4 in. Directed by José E. Pintor. New York: Premium Latin Music Inc, 2010.

Sedgwick, Eve Kosofsky. *Between Men: English Literature and Male Homosocial Desire*. New York: Columbia University Press, 1985.

———. *Epistemology of the Closet*. Berkeley: University of California Press, 1990.

Sención Silverio, Lorenzo and Abelardo Freites-Báez. *Academia Militar "Batalla De Las Carreras": Apuntes históricos y anecdóticos*. 1st ed. Santo Domingo, República Dominicana: Editora de Luxe, 2006.

Simmons, Kimberly Eison. *Reconstructing Racial Identity and the African Past in the Dominican Republic*. Gainesville, FL: University Press of Florida, 2009.

Stinchcomb, Dawn F. *The Development of Literary Blackness in the Dominican Republic*. Gainesville: University Press of Florida, 2004.

Torres-Saillant, Silvio. *El tigueraje intelectual*. Santo Domingo, República Dominicana: Sociedad Editorial Dominicana, 2002.

———. *Introduction to Dominican Blackness*. New York: CUNY Dominican Studies Institute at the City College of New York, 1999.

Notes on Contributors

Josep M. Armengol-Carrera obtained his Ph.D. in English from the University of Barcelona, Spain, with the thesis "Gendering Men: Theorizing Masculinities in American Culture and Literature" (2006). A renowned masculinity scholar, he has lectured and published extensively on masculinity studies, especially on literary representations of masculinity, in prestigious academic journals such as *Signs*, *Men and Masculinities*, the *Hemingway Review*, and *Journal of Men's Studies*, among others. His latest books include *Debating Masculinity* (2009), *Richard Ford and the Fiction of Masculinities* (the winner of the 2010 Literary Scholarship Prize awarded annually by the Spanish Association for Anglo-American Studies), and *Men in Color: Racialized Masculinities in U.S. Literature and Cinema* (2011). He is also an international advisory editor for the academic journal *Men and Masculinities* (Sage Publications), as well as co-editor of the "Masculinity Studies" series at Peter Lang. Currently, he is Associate Professor of English at the University of Castilla-La Mancha, Spain, where he is working on a new book on masculinities in African American fiction.

After studying Non-Western English Literature and Latin American & Caribbean Studies at Hunter College, CUNY, **Danny M. Barreto** received his Ph.D. in Hispanic Languages & Literature in 2010 from Stony Brook University, SUNY, where he also completed a graduate program in Women's Studies. His doctoral research centered on issues of family, gender, and nation in late-nineteenth-century Galician narrative. Since then he has broadened his work on the modern regionalist novel, gender and sexuality, and Galician Studies to also include transatlantic emigrant literature, twentieth- and twenty-first century Galician literature and film, and post-national approaches to modern Spanish literature. At Stony Brook University and Brooklyn College, he taught classes on a range of subjects including feminist theory, Spanish Gothic literature and film, Puerto Rican literature, urban landscapes in narratives from Spain and Latin America, and ghosts and *desaparecidos* in Latin American narrative. He is now an Adjunct Assistant Professor in the Department of Hispanic Studies at Vassar College, New York, where he teaches courses on nineteenth- to twenty-first-century Spanish literature, as well as Spanish and Latin American languages and cultures.

José R. Cartagena-Calderón (Ph.D. Harvard University) is Associate Professor of Romance Languages and Literatures at Pomona College. He is the author of *Masculinidades en obras: el drama de la hombría en la España imperial* (2008) and of numerous articles on the literary and cultural production of Spain and the Americas from the late 15th through the 17th centuries. His research addresses the need in literary and cultural studies for more elaborate understandings of the relations of various masculinities to power, empire, ethnicity, class, and sexuality in historically specific contexts. He is currently working on a book project on the intersection of homoeroticism and the sacred in early modern Spain.

Jaume Martí-Olivella is Associate Professor in the Languages, Literatures and Cultures Department at the University of New Hampshire. He is the co-founder of CINE-LIT, an international conference on Hispanic cinema and literature. He is also co-founder and former president of the North American Catalan Society. He has published *Basque Cinema An Introduction* (2003). He has co-edited the volume *Spain Is (Still) Different: Tourism and Discourse in Spanish Identity.* (2008). He has also co-edited five *CINE-LIT Proceedings* (1992, 1995, 1998, 2001, 2003), two special issues of *Latin American Issues* on "The Caribbean(s) Redefined" (1997) and "(De)Constructing the Mexican-American Border" (1998), and two special issues of *Catalan Review* on "Woman, History and Nation in the Works of Montserrat Roig and Maria Aurèlia Capmany (1993) and " Homage to Mercè Rodoreda" (1988). He has also published numerous articles on Hispanic cinema and cultural studies. Currently, he is completing two book manuscripts: *Basque Cinema: The Shining Paradox* and *Contemporary Catalan Cinema: Catalonia's New Gaze.*

Begoña Regueiro-Salgado holds a PhD in Spanish literature, with the thesis "The Poetics of the Second Romanticism in Spain." Since 2005 she has been working in the Spanish literature Department of the Universidad Complutense de Madrid. Currently, she is also teaching in the Language and Literature Department of the Faculty of Education of the Universidad Complutense. Her main research lines are nineteenth-century Spanish literature, nineteenth- and twentieth-century Galician literature, women writers and gender relations in the nineteenth century, and digital poetry in Spanish. She is the author of *La poética del Segundo Romanticismo* (2010) and has edited the book *Realidad y literatura en las letras hispánicas* (2009). She has also published numerous articles and book chapters on nineteenth-century Spanish literature, particularly on women writers and the Second Romantics.

Elena Valdez is a doctoral student at Rutgers, the State University of New Jersey. Her research interests include Hispanic Caribbean literature, twentieth- and twenty-first-century Latin American narrative, gender studies, and queer theory. Within the Hispanic Caribbean narrative, her principal interests are queer sexuality, urban space, and national identity. She has published articles on urban space and queer sexuality in the Caribbean in several scholarly journals, including *Letras Hispanas* and *OsaMayor*. She is currently teaching at Swarthmore College.

MASCULINITY STUDIES

Literary and Cultural Representations

Josep M. Armengol-Carrera and Àngels Carabí
General Editors

In line with the latest trends within masculinity scholarship, the books appearing in the Masculinity Studies series deal with representations of masculinities in culture, in general, and literature, in particular. The aim of this series is twofold. On the one hand, it focuses on studies that question traditionally normative representations of masculinities. On the other, it seeks to highlight new alternative representations of manhood, looking for more egalitarian models of manhood in and through literature and culture. Besides literary representations, the series is open to studies of masculinity in cinema, theatre, music, as well as all kinds of artistic and visual representations.

For further information about the series and submitting manuscripts, please contact:

Peter Lang Publishing, Inc.
Acquisitions Department
29 Broadway, 18th floor
New York, New York 10006

To order, please contact our Customer Service Department at:

800-770-LANG (within the U.S.)
212-647-7706 (outside the U.S.)
212-647-7707 FAX
CustomerService@plang.com

Or browse online by series at:
www.peterlang.com